20.95

SCIENTISTS

ENRICO FERMI

TRAILBLAZER IN NUCLEAR PHYSICS

Erica Stux

Enslow Publishers, Inc.

40 Industrial Road   PO Box 38
Box 398   Aldershot
Berkeley Heights, NJ 07922   Hants GU12 6BP
USA   UK

http://www.enslow.com

"Along with Fermi's significant discoveries, and to a certain extent equivalent, can be placed his experimental skill, his brilliant inventiveness, and his intuition."

—Professor H. Pleijel

I am grateful to my husband Bill Shore who was very helpful with suggestions and encouragement during the writing of this book.

Copyright © 2004 by Erica Stux

Library of Congress Cataloging-in-Publication Data

Stux, Erica.
    Enrico Fermi : trailblazer in nuclear physics / Erica Stux.
        v. cm. — (Nobel Prize-winning scientists)
    Includes bibliographical references and index.
    Contents: What's inside an atom? — Early years — Preparing for a career — Bringing modern physics to Italy — Experiments on atomic nuclei — Momentous changes — The war effort — Chicago and Los Alamos— After the war — Fermi's legacy.
    ISBN 0-7660-2177-7
    1. Fermi, Enrico, 1901-1954—Juvenile literature. 2. Nuclear physicists—Italy—Biography—Juvenile literature. [1. Fermi, Enrico, 1901-1954. 2. Nuclear physicists. 3. Scientists. 4. Nobel Prizes—Biography.] I. Title. II. Series.
    QC774.F4S78 2004
    530'.092—dc21

                  2003001283

Printed in the United States of America

10 9 8 7 6 5 4 3 2 1

Illustration Credits: © The Nobel Foundation, p. 5, ArtToday.com, pp. 9, 109; Courtesy of Rachel Fermi, pp. 19, 29, 40, 43, 51, 67, 79, 89; Enslow Publishers, Inc., pp. 13, 75, 93; National Archives, pp. 86, 99.

Cover Illustration: Corel Corporation (background); ArtToday.com (foreground).

CONTENTS

THE NOBEL PRIZE

Every year since its founding in 1901, the Nobel Prize has been awarded to individuals who have distinguished themselves in the fields of physiology or medicine, physics, chemistry, literature, and peace. (In 1968 a prize for economics was added.) The prize is named for Alfred Nobel, a Swede born in Stockholm in 1833, who grew up to become a successful chemist, manufacturer, and businessman.

Nobel began experimenting with ways to make nitroglycerine safer for practical use. Eventually he found a way to mix nitroglycerine with silica and make a paste. He could then shape the paste into a stick that could be placed in holes drilled in rocks. He patented this creation in 1867 and named it dynamite. In order to detonate the dynamite sticks, Nobel also invented a blasting cap that could be ignited by burning a fuse. The invention of dynamite, along with equipment like the diamond drilling crown and the pneumatic drill, significantly reduced the expenses associated with many types of construction work.

Soon Nobel's dynamite and blasting caps were in great demand. Nobel proved to be an astute businessman, establishing companies and laboratories throughout the world. He also continued to experiment with other chemical inventions and held more than 350 patents in his lifetime.

Alfred Nobel did not narrow his learning just to scientific knowledge. His love of literature and poetry prompted him to write his own works, and his social conscience kept him interested in peace-related issues.

When Nobel died on December 10, 1896, and his will was read, everyone was surprised to learn that he left instructions that the accumulated fortune from his companies and business ventures (estimated at more than $3 million U.S.) was to be used to award prizes in physics, chemistry, physiology or medicine, literature, and peace.

In fulfilling Alfred Nobel's will, the Nobel Foundation was established in order to oversee the funds left by Nobel and to coordinate the work of the prize-awarding institutions. Nobel prizes are presented every December 10, the anniversary of Alfred Nobel's death.

CHAPTER ONE

WHAT'S INSIDE AN ATOM?

Enrico Fermi sat near his telephone the evening of November 10, 1938. He had been told earlier that day to expect a call from Stockholm, Sweden. That could mean only one thing: he had been chosen to receive the Nobel Prize.

His mind worked feverishly. The importance of his work was going to be recognized—this was exciting enough. But in addition, this would provide him and his family with a long-awaited opportunity. From Stockholm, they would go directly to the United States. They would leave their native Italy, with its hateful form of government headed by the dictator Benito Mussolini. Mussolini, leader of the Fascist party, had taken over the government in 1922. Fascism promised social justice for downtrodden citizens, but also sought to control all aspects of life. It was opposed to the concept of democracy.

For several days in October 1922, Italy had been in turmoil, hovering on the brink of civil war. To avoid a war, the king made Mussolini premier. Mussolini's associates were put into key government posts. Fascist thugs were then allowed to roam the streets and beat up elected officials. Slowly, through a policy of terror, Mussolini consolidated his power. The Fascist party became the only legal political party. Newspapers were told what they could and could not print. The king remained, but just for show—he had no real power.

Fermi had realized even then that opportunities for young people would be limited in Italy. Perhaps, he thought, he would be better off somewhere else. These feelings grew in the late 1930s, when Italy, following the lead of its ally Germany, passed laws restricting the rights of its Jewish citizens. Even if Fermi's wife Laura had not been Jewish, he knew he could never support a government that was so repressive. But he concentrated on his career and waited for an opportunity to leave Italy. With the call from Stockholm, that opportunity was now at hand.

During the next four weeks the Fermi family made preparations to leave their homeland. Because he already had a reputation in scientific circles, Fermi was sure he could find an American university where he could continue his research.

The early twentieth century was an exciting time for physicists. Whereas from ancient times certain individuals called alchemists had attempted to turn common

NOBEL PRIZE-WINNING SCIENTIST ENRICO FERMI DRAWS ON A BLACK-BOARD DURING A LECTURE.

metals like lead into gold or silver, it was not until the twentieth century that a way was found to turn one element into another. However, the goal of these recent experiments was not to obtain gold or silver. Rather, these experiments were conducted for the purpose of studying atomic behavior.

Among the ancient Greeks, some philosophers believed that all substances are made up of tiny indivisible particles that the Greek Democritus called *atoms* (from *a*, meaning "not," and *tomos*, meaning "divisible or sliceable"). An atom is the smallest particle of an element that can exist alone. Modern calculations put the diameter of an atom at 0.00000001 centimeters. One inch can cover 250 million atoms.[1]

There are 92 naturally occurring elements, from hydrogen, the lightest, to uranium, the heaviest. In 1808 an English scientist, John Dalton, proposed that all atoms of an element have the same size and weight. The Russian chemist Dimitri Ivanovich Mendeleev drew up a chart of the elements in 1869, grouping together those elements with similar properties. He even predicted the existence of then-unknown elements to fill gaps in his chart.

In 1897 the English physicist J. J. Thomson showed that tiny negatively charged particles he called electrons can be given off by atoms, leaving behind positively charged units in what was later called the nucleus of the atom. These positively charged units found in the nucleus were called protons. The atomic number that

Mendeleev had assigned to each element represents the number of protons in the atom of the element.

Some heavy elements were found to give off particles spontaneously, with no outside force acting on them. This process is called radioactivity. It was first observed in uranium in 1896 by the French physicist Antoine Henri Becquerel. Marie Curie and her husband, Pierre, investigated radioactivity in other heavy elements. For this work, Becquerel and the Curies shared the Nobel Prize in physics in 1903. The products of radiation given off by radioactive elements are known as alpha particles, beta particles, and gamma rays, which are similar to X-rays. "What are these particles?" physicists asked themselves. "What is inside an atom, and how can an atom's behavior be explained?"

What is inside an atom, and how can an atom's behavior be explained?

For centuries, scientists tried to explain the world around them by observation and experiment. The Italian astronomer Galileo, for example, proved that falling bodies fall at the same rate by dropping them from a tower. The Englishman Isaac Newton showed that light is made up of all colors of the rainbow by passing a beam through a glass prism. But Newton also used mathematics to reason about things without doing experiments. He was the first great theoretician. As scientific knowledge grew, most physicists found that the field was much too broad for them to absorb everything. They became either experimentalists or theoreticians. A theoretician works out relationships between quantities mathematically. Then, others test the theory by experimentation. If the math predicted correctly what happened in the experiment, then the theory is correct. If not, more calculations may be necessary. Many physicists in the early twentieth century turned to mathematics to work out theories about the structure and behavior of atoms.

Many found, however, that the old laws of physics did not apply when studying something as small as an atom. An entirely new set of rules had to be worked out. Some of these rules seemed to be quite contradictory. For example, some of the particles that make up atoms can behave like waves, similar to light. Conversely, Albert Einstein in 1905 proposed that light waves are made up of particles called photons. It all depends on how an experiment is carried out. In one kind of experiment, light acts as waves; in another, it acts as particles. Therefore we can say that characteristics of both are exhibited. The rules that describe these phenomena are called quantum theory. Furthermore, Einstein, basing his work on earlier ideas of the German physicist Max Planck, stated that all radiation (gamma rays, X-rays, light, microwaves, radio waves) consists of photons. We can think of photons as tiny packets of energy.

A New Zealand physicist, Ernest Rutherford, proposed in 1911 that an atom's structure consists of a central nucleus surrounded by electrons. The Danish physicist Niels Bohr expanded on this by proposing that electrons move only in certain orbits around the nucleus, depending on their energy levels. They can absorb energy, and in doing so move into a larger orbit. They can then give off this extra energy in the form of light or other radiation, and drop back into their original orbit.

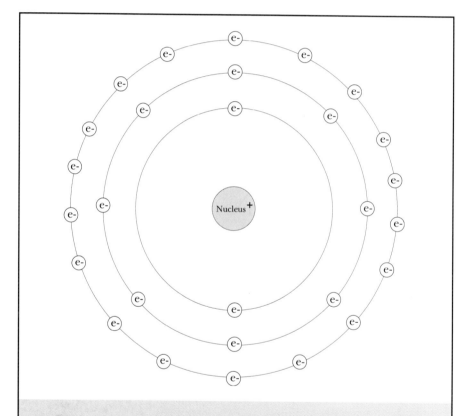

THE BOHR MODEL OF THE ATOM PROPOSED THAT NEGATIVELY CHARGED ELECTRONS CIRCLED THE POSITIVELY CHARGED NUCLEUS IN DIFFERENT LEVELS. THE FIRST LEVEL OUTSIDE THE NUCLEUS COULD CONTAIN A MAXIMUM OF TWO ELECTRONS; THE SECOND LEVEL EIGHT ELECTRONS; AND THE THIRD LEVEL EIGHTEEN.

Gradually physicists thought they were beginning to understand what happens inside an atom. But surprises were still ahead. They found that in some experiments certain elements were transformed into entirely different elements. The goal of the alchemists of old was being achieved, in a way.

Enrico Fermi was interested in radioactivity. He was the rare kind of physicist who was skilled at both developing theories and carrying out experiments. Like most scientists, he built on and extended work that had already been done. He wondered whether all the elements could be made radioactive, and so he carried out systematic investigations. He found that many did undergo such transformations. In his Nobel Prize acceptance speech, he stated, "Out of 63 elements investigated, 37 showed an easily detectable activity. The percentage of the activatable elements did not show any marked dependence on the atomic weight of the element."[2] In other words, light elements could be made radioactive as well as heavy ones. Uranium and thorium showed especially strong activity when bombarded with neutrons. But in the case of uranium, the products were difficult to identify. Fermi and his team concluded that they had produced elements 93 and 94. Later on it was discovered that this conclusion was false. Eventually, the discovery of the process called fission would explain what was happening to the uranium.

In presenting Fermi to the Royal Swedish Academy of Sciences and to the Swedish king, Professor H. Pleijel stated, "Along with Fermi's significant discoveries, and to a certain extent equivalent, can be placed his experimental skill, his brilliant inventiveness, and his intuition. These qualities have found expression in the creation of refined research methods which made it possible to demonstrate the existence of these newly formed substances, which occur in extremely small quantities."[3]

At that time, the significance of Fermi's discoveries were not fully appreciated. Just seven years later they were to usher in the Atomic Age.

CHAPTER TWO

EARLY YEARS

For centuries the Fermi family had been peasants. Enrico's grandfather, Stefano, was the first of the family to give up farming. He was employed by the Duke of Parma. Parma was then one of the small independent states that were later united to form the nation of Italy. Enrico's grandmother was a typical nineteenth-century Italian woman—a good housewife with many domestic skills, devoted to her family and to the Catholic Church. Though she could read, she never learned to write.

The Fermis' children were encouraged to care for themselves at an early age. Their second son, Alberto, would become the father of Enrico. He probably attended a technical high school before going to work for a railroad company. His ambition and determination allowed him to rise in rank to the position of division head.

Alberto settled in Rome and married Ida de Gattis, a schoolteacher, in 1898. He was forty-one and she was twenty-seven.[1] The couple lived in an apartment in a part of town that had been built up rapidly when Rome became the capital of Italy in 1870. A daughter named Maria was born in 1899; a son, Giulio, came in 1900; and Enrico was born on September 29, 1901. Because Mrs. Fermi could not care for all three babies, Enrico and Giulio were sent to live with nurses in the countryside—a common practice in Europe at that time. Enrico did not return to his parents until he was two-and-a-half. He adjusted quickly to his family. Mrs. Fermi treated her children with affection, but she also held them to high moral and intellectual standards.[2] However, they were not raised in the strict religious tradition of the Fermi grandparents.

The building they lived in had no central heating, and their apartment had no hot water. For their daily bathing, the family used two zinc tubs. The tubs were wheeled into the bedrooms at night and filled with cold water so that by morning the water reached room temperature. The three children plunged into the water each morning, no matter how cold it might still be. They were taught that persons of peasant stock needed to be strong.[3] Later, Enrico would tell how he used to sit on his hands while studying in order to keep them warm.

Enrico could already read and write when he started school at age six. Early on he showed an aptitude for mathematics and also demonstrated an unusually good memory. He could recite long passages of poetry from memory.[4] Because he learned his lessons rapidly, he had more free time, which he used for further reading in math and science. He was not just a bookworm, though.

He also loved sports, and his competitive spirit drove him to try to be the best. He hated to lose at any game. This drive remained with him his whole life.

Enrico's closest friend and constant companion was his brother, Giulio. Together they built little mechanical toys and electric motors. Enrico was shy and quiet as a youngster, whereas Giulio was friendlier and was thought to be the more intelligent of the two.[5]

Tragedy stuck the Fermi family when Enrico was thirteen. Giulio went to the hospital for a routine operation to remove a throat abscess. But while he was on the operating table, he died. Ida Fermi never recovered from the shock of losing Giulio. Enrico, unable to express his feelings of grief, buried himself in his books. Although he still played outdoor games with other boys, his heart was not in them.

Soon he found a new friend, a schoolmate named Enrico Persico. The two realized they had much in common—a natural curiosity about the world and scientific aptitude. Their temperaments were different, though; Enrico Fermi was now self-assured, whereas Persico was cautious and shy. They fell into the habit of taking walks together and discussing all kinds of subjects. Persico admired his new friend greatly. Enrico Fermi, he wrote later, "brought a precision of ideas, a self-assurance, and an originality which continually surprised me. In mathematics and in physics he showed knowledge of many subjects well beyond what was taught at school. He

Enrico Fermi as a young boy with his brother, Giulio (left).

knew these topics . . . in such a way that he could use them . . ."[6]

Sometimes the two Enricos walked to Rome's outdoor market to look over the secondhand books for sale. Here Fermi found a book that covered mechanics, optics, acoustics, and astronomy as these subjects were known in 1840, the year the book was published. At home he pored over the text and mathematical symbols, hardly noticing that it was written in Latin. His study of Latin grammar and vocabulary at school had paid off. He enthusiastically passed on to his friend all of his new-found knowledge.

The two boys carried out experiments, using whatever equipment they could lay their hands on. They made measurements of various things, such as the magnetic field of the earth. One problem that puzzled them was how to explain the motion of a top. Tops were popular toys among young boys. Why does a spinning top remain vertical, they wondered. And why, when it slows down, does the upper part move in a circle? At what speed does this happen?[7] This problem occupied both boys for a long time. Fermi finally solved it, using mathematics.

That same year Enrico acquired another friend, this one an adult. Enrico was in the habit of meeting his father, Alberto Fermi, when he finished work each day, and walking home with him. This togetherness helped them cope with the loss of Giulio. Often they were joined by Adolfo Amidei, a co-worker of Alberto's. Upon learning that Amidei was well-versed in physics and math, Enrico peppered him with questions. Amidei was impressed by the boy's interest in science and his ability to think clearly. He lent Enrico a book on projective geometry, which explained how this branch of math could be used. Enrico returned it after two months, saying he had solved all the problems at the end of the book. A surprised Amidei asked to see Enrico's work, since he himself had found some of the problems rather difficult. Enrico proved to him that he had indeed done all the problems.

During the next three years, Amidei lent Enrico books on various branches of mathematics: algebra, trigonometry, analytical geometry, and calculus. Enrico studied the contents of these books avidly, and worked out all the problems in each book before returning it. Amidei told him he could keep the calculus book longer, in case he needed to refer to it later. Enrico thanked him, saying, "That won't be necessary. . . . As a matter of fact, after a few years I'll see the concepts in it even more clearly than now, and if I need a formula, I'll know how to derive it easily enough."[8] Now Amidei was really impressed!

The Italian school system consisted of elementary school, followed by five years of middle school. At fifteen, a student could go to a technical school or to a liceo, which was a three-year program that prepared students for university studies. In July 1918 Enrico graduated from the liceo, after being allowed to skip the third year. Now he faced the question of which university to enroll in. Amidei asked him whether he preferred to concentrate on physics or math. Enrico answered, "I studied mathematics with passion because I considered it necessary for the study of physics, to which I want to dedicate myself exclusively."[9]

Amidei recommended that Enrico enroll at the University of Pisa—but only after first gaining admission at the Scuola Normale Superiore in Pisa. There he could have room and board, and he could attend classes at both institutions. In the meantime, Amidei suggested that Enrico study German, since many scientific papers were written in that language.

Enrico's parents did not approve of his plan to study in Pisa. They had already lost one son, and now the other one was planning to leave for four years. Why could he not stay home and attend classes at the University of Rome? But Amidei pointed out the advantages of going to Pisa: it would be preparation for a brilliant career. The Scuola Normale accepted only forty of the brightest young men of Italy. Surely Enrico would be among those.

> "I studied mathematics with passion because I considered it necessary for the study of physics, to which I want to dedicate myself exclusively."
>
> —Enrico Fermi

On November 14, 1918, Enrico took the entrance exam for admission to the Scuola Normale. His essay topic was "The Characteristics of Sound." He poured everything he knew into his essay, even using higher mathematics in his explanations. The examiner was surprised to find so much knowledge in a young man of seventeen. He called Enrico into his office, and told him he was sure to win a scholarship. Also, he said, Enrico had the ability to some day become an important scientist.

Soon after that, Enrico left the bustling city of Rome and moved to the quiet town of Pisa, whose glory days were long gone. The four years he spent there proved to be among the happiest of Enrico Fermi's life.

CHAPTER THREE

PREPARING FOR A CAREER

Pisa had been one of the great cities of the late Middle Ages. The city was a leader in art, literature, and science. While some of its splendor faded over the centuries, the University of Pisa in the late 1800s still attracted leaders in the fields of mathematics and the humanities.

The Scuola Normale Superiore had been established by Napoleon in 1810 as a branch of the university. Its aim was to train teachers and promote research. Its elite student body was a major source of talent in Italy. By the time Fermi arrived in November 1918, a feeling of relief and confidence in the future pervaded the country, because the First World War was ending and a long-lasting peace was in sight.

The Scuola was housed in a sixteenth-century palace, not far from the famous Leaning Tower of Pisa. The elegantly adorned palace exterior contrasted with the bareness of the students' rooms. There was no heating system, and little furniture for the students. Heat was provided by burning charcoal in a crockpot in each room. Male stewards served meals and took care of cleaning the rooms.[1]

The forty students were divided into two groups: humanities, and math and science. Whereas all took their studies seriously, they also found time for bicycling and hiking in the nearby mountains. Fermi plunged into the lighter side of student life. Perhaps he was glad to escape the gloomy atmosphere that had pervaded his home ever since Giulio's death.[2] Because mosquitoes were a constant summertime nuisance, Fermi became adept at shooting elastic garters (used to hold up socks) at them. He claimed to be the best mosquito killer in the school.

Soon after his arrival, Fermi became friends with Franco Rasetti, a physics student, who lived at home with his mother. Rasetti's main interest was nature. He collected plants and insects, and classified them. But rather than register in the biology department, he chose physics because he knew that would present a challenge. Rasetti liked challenges but had little interest in people, and delighted in playing tricks on others. He organized a group of students into an "Anti-Neighbors Society." Fermi gleefully joined in the fun. Among their tricks was placing a pan of water on top of a partly-closed door, so that the first person opening the door would get a shower.[3] Another prank was to attach a small padlock through the buttonholes of an unsuspecting victim. One time Fermi and Rasetti exploded a stink bomb during a lecture. For this they were almost expelled. Only the intervention of their physics professor saved them.

Members of the Anti-Neighbors Society also played tricks on each other. Once Fermi got up early and walked to Rasetti's house. He took two screw eyelets out of his pocket and attached one to the front door and the other to the door frame. Then he snapped a padlock through them. Rasetti awoke to find himself a prisoner in his own house. Fortunately, this did not dampen their friendship. Fermi was often invited to dinner at Rasetti's house. Mrs. Rasetti's cooking was a welcome change from the meals served at the school.

Besides his studies connected with classwork, Fermi devoted much thought to the basic concepts of physics. During the summer vacation of 1919 he decided to organize his knowledge of physics. He entered in a notebook everything he knew on such topics as magnetism, radioactivity, and electrical properties of gases, among others. He put in math problems, too, some of which were quite difficult. The notes were written in pencil, with almost no erasures. The notebook showed an amazing grasp of physics for someone who had only completed one year of university study.

Fermi's abilities were very soon recognized by his professors, as well as by other students. He wrote to his friend Persico in January 1920: "At the physics department I am slowly becoming the most influential authority."[4] By the following year, he had mastered German, which he could speak fairly well, and English, which he could read in scientific journals. He had already learned French in high school.

After two years in Pisa, Fermi, Rasetti, and one other student were accepted into the physics department for advanced work. This would be comparable to graduate school at an American university today. The three made up the entire department, and were allowed to do whatever research they wanted. Since X-ray equipment was available and he had already done some reading about X-rays, Fermi decided to use it for research. However, this equipment proved to be unsatisfactory, and the three students had to build various parts themselves. Although it was inconvenient, this building of equipment gave Fermi valuable experience. In his future projects he often found it necessary to construct his own instruments.

Fermi published the first of several theoretical papers in January 1921. But when it came to choosing a topic for research leading to a doctor's degree, he chose experimental work on X-rays. The reason was that theoretical physics was not recognized by Italian universities as an acceptable topic at the time. Fermi loved experimental work just as much as theoretical, and he enjoyed alternating between the two.[5] His research dealt with X-ray diffraction by crystals of various substances. When X-rays are passed through a crystal, their path is bent by interaction with the individual atoms of the crystal. This produces a characteristic pattern of spots on photographic film and indicates the internal structure of the crystal.

As was the custom, the candidate for the degree had to speak about his work before a faculty committee. Eleven examiners dressed in black robes gathered to listen to Fermi. His knowledge overwhelmed them. Some suppressed yawns, others relaxed and did not even try to follow his explanations. He received his doctor's degree with high honors in July 1922, two months before his twenty-first birthday. However, his thesis was controversial and the university, which usually published the work of its doctoral graduates, refused to publish Fermi's work.[6]

At about the same time, Fermi had to present a paper to the Scuola Normale. This one dealt with probability and its applications to astronomy. Later that year he published a paper that dealt mathematically with Einstein's theory of relativity. This theory was a revolutionary way of looking at the world: that space and time are not independent of each other, and that mass and energy are interchangeable. This paper gave Fermi such a reputation that in 1923 he was invited to write an essay to be included in a book on relativity. At twenty-two he was already recognized as an authority.[7]

Fermi returned to his family in Rome after completing his studies. For guidance in his career, he sought out Professor Orso Mario Corbino, a prominent physicist at the University of Rome. Besides being a professor, Corbino was also a senator—an appointment that carried both political and academic distinction. This gave him influence in government circles.

ENRICO FERMI DURING HIS DAYS AS A COLLEGE PROFESSOR IN ITALY.

Fermi was in Corbino's office when events occurred that changed the course of his life. On October 28, 1922, Fascist soldiers entered Rome. The black-shirted young men closed some streets with rolls of barbed wire, and stationed armed guards at certain corners. The Italian cabinet announced "a state of siege." That meant that the army was instructed to resist the Fascists. But the army would do nothing until the king signed a document proclaiming a state of siege. The king, fearing a civil war, refused to do this.

On that particular morning, Fermi and Corbino did not talk about physics. Politics and the present situation dominated their conversation. Corbino considered the Fascists, led by Benito Mussolini, to be dangerous to the stability of Italy.

"If the king signs it [the decree], we may have a civil war," he told Fermi.

"Do you think he may go against his cabinet?" Fermi asked. "He has never been known to take the lead, but has always followed his ministers."

Corbino paused, then said, "Yes, I think there is a chance that the king may not sign the decree. He is a man of courage."

"Then there is still a hope."

"Hope? Of what? Not of salvation. If the king doesn't sign, we are certainly going to have a Fascist dictatorship under Mussolini."[8]

That evening, Fermi repeated this conversation to his family. A dictatorship, he told them, would mean that young people like himself would have to emigrate—that is, leave Italy for another country.

In the meantime, Fermi wanted to become a professor at a leading university. But at that time there were no openings. So he did what many scientists do: he went abroad for further study, to the University of Göttingen in Germany. His knowledge of German made the move an easy one. The Italian Ministry of Public Instruction sent him money each week for his living expenses. After several months, he used his savings to buy a bicycle.

Fermi was shy and felt like an outsider at Göttingen. Although his professor, a well-known physicist named Max Born, was hospitable, Fermi felt he did not belong in the professor's circle. Although he had built up a reputation in Italy, Fermi was relatively unknown in Germany. At the end of the academic year, he returned to Rome, and began teaching math courses at the University of Rome. This was only a temporary position.

A paper Fermi had written the previous year came to the attention of Paul Ehrenfest, a physicist at the University of Leyden in Holland. Ehrenfest invited Fermi to Leyden on a three-month scholarship. He gave Fermi encouragement and reassurance. It meant a lot to Fermi that Ehrenfest appreciated his talents.

After Leyden, Fermi took another temporary position at the University of Florence, where he taught theoretical mechanics and electricity. Fermi was happy to team up again with his friend Rasetti, who was already at Florence. The two could discuss and plan experiments together. Fermi was better at theory and Rasetti was better at experimentation. They undertook a project to measure the frequency of radiation of mercury when a weak magnetic field is applied. Fermi knew that when an electric current—that is, a beam of electrons—is passed through a tube containing mercury vapor, the electrons are absorbed by mercury atoms, which immediately give off photons. This is the principle underlying the mercury vapor lamps that are now common along highways. Since an electric current produces a magnetic field, and vice versa, Fermi and Rasetti used a magnetic field to discover how the frequency of the emitted photons—that is, the color of the light emitted—varies with the strength of the magnetic field. They found some suitable equipment in the laboratory, but built several components themselves. The budget for new equipment was almost nonexistent.

Publication in the most widely-read scientific journals is important to any scientist. In Italy, the Fascist government insisted that all scientific work be published in Italian journals. However, these were rarely read outside of Italy. Therefore Fermi sent what he felt was important work to Germany to be published in the leading German journals. In this way he could enhance his international reputation. Less important work could be published in Italy only. Later, in the 1930s, he abandoned publishing in German, to protest against the Nazi government in Germany, and instead concentrated on English-language journals.

Fermi wanted to make lasting contributions in physics,

but to do that he needed a university career. He needed to pull a few strings to get a permanent university appointment. Luckily that opportunity came in the fall of 1925.

Professor Corbino had ambitious dreams for his department at the University of Rome. Italy had been the center of scientific advances from the time of Galileo in the seventeenth century to the time of the physicist Volta in the late eighteenth century. Since then, however, the lead had passed to other countries. Corbino was determined to change this. He hoped to attract to his department talented young men who could do significant research and perhaps make great discoveries. In this way he hoped his school would gain recognition all over the world. Corbino himself had abandoned research, after achieving some stature in the field. He had turned to politics and been appointed to a cabinet post. When the king asked Mussolini to form a new government, Corbino was again asked to take a post in the cabinet, even though he had not joined the Fascist party.

"At the physics department I am slowly becoming the most influential authority."
—Enrico Fermi

Italian law held that any vacancy on a university faculty had to be filled by holding a competition among applicants. A committee of professors from several universities chose applicants based on their teaching record and their publications. Three candidates were chosen. The first choice was to fill the position at the university that had the vacancy. The other two could fill vacancies at other universities as they occurred.[9]

When the University of Cagliari on the island of Sardinia announced a competition for a faculty position in 1925, Fermi decided to apply. Though Cagliari is rather remote from the Italian mainland, a position there could be a stepping-stone to better positions. Fermi felt he had a good chance because he had already published thirty scientific papers. Most of these were theoretical studies in the field of relativity—mathematical treatments based on speculation and assumptions. Not everyone at that time accepted Einstein's theory of relativity. Of the five examiners for the Cagliari post, two were pro-Einstein and favored Fermi. But the other three favored an older man, who was then appointed to the vacancy.

Thus Fermi was still teaching in Florence when Corbino thought of bringing him into his department in Rome. His reputation had grown over the past year. He had been interested in statistical questions—that is, a mathematical explanation of the behavior of atoms and electrons. It was a time when many new theories were advanced in the study of atomic physics.

Wolfgang Pauli, an Austrian physicist, had discovered in 1925 the principle of exclusion, which says that in each orbit (or at each energy level) of the nucleus of an atom, there can be at most two electrons, but these must have opposite spins. Fermi extended this principle. He showed mathematically that no two atoms of a gas can move with exactly the same velocity.[10] His calculations became known as Fermi-Dirac statistics. (Paul Dirac arrived at similar results.) When this paper was published in a German journal, it proved to be Fermi's first major contribution. It became important in the development of theoretical physics.

Fermi easily won the competition for the new post of professor of theoretical physics at the University of Rome. The committee stated that it "unanimously recognized [Professor Fermi's] exceptional qualities and finds that he, even at his young age and after very few years of scientific activity, already highly honors Italian physics."[11]

CHAPTER FOUR

BRINGING MODERN PHYSICS TO ITALY

In addition to his teaching and research work, Fermi found time for fun. In Florence he and his friend Rasetti spent hours lying in a grassy field, trying to catch little lizards. Their aim was to let them loose in the university dining hall in order to scare the girls who waited on the tables. But even while he held a long glass rod with a little lasso at the end, waiting for a lizard to approach, Fermi's mind was working on some scientific theory, like trying to explain the behavior of a certain gas.

Hiking in the hills outside Rome was a favorite pastime among young people. In the spring of 1924 a sixteen-year-old named Laura Capon was persuaded by her friends to join a group of hikers. She was introduced to Enrico Fermi, who seemed to be the leader of the group. Her friends told her, "He is a promising physicist, already teaching at the university, although he is only twenty-two."[1]

Two years passed before Laura and Enrico met again. Laura's family vacationed in a picturesque valley of Italy's Dolomite Mountains in 1926. Fermi also happened to be staying nearby. Laura felt more at ease with him than she had the first time they met. Fermi took charge of the young people from various vacationing families and planned daily hikes into the mountains. Tirelessly he shepherded his little group up steep trails, sometimes falling back to encourage the slower ones. While regaining his lead, he bounced his backpack playfully against those he passed. When anyone protested his strenuous pace, he claimed that his legs, or his heart and lungs, were custom-made.

With vacation time over, everyone returned to the city. Laura found herself eagerly awaiting news about Fermi from any of her friends. But thoughts of marriage never crossed her mind. Fermi had once described his ideal wife as tall, blond, and athletic, with four living grandparents. Laura did not fit any of these criteria.

Some time in 1927, Fermi told his friends that he felt like doing something extravagant, something not in keeping with his thrifty ways. He would either purchase a car, or take a wife. The car came first—a tiny yellow Peugeot, into which he packed his friends for Sunday drives around the countryside. Other friends would follow in Rasetti's car. Two or three would have to sit in the Peugeot's rumble seat. Laura did not mind this in fine weather, but when it rained, "the rumble became a humiliating wet hole."[2]

Sometimes one of the two cars stalled. Then the passengers had to wait by the side of the road while Fermi and Rasetti fumbled with wires under the hood. Somehow they always got the car running again.

Enrico Fermi ignored Laura's shortcomings as his "ideal" wife. The two were married on July 19, 1928. Their wedding day was unusually hot. Friends and relatives gathered at Laura's parents' home in the morning. They would proceed in a group to City Hall. The wedding was to be a civil ceremony because of the different religions of the bride and groom—Catholicism for Fermi and Judaism for Laura—though neither family was particularly religious.

For their wedding trip, the couple flew to Genoa in an eight-passenger seaplane. As it skirted the shoreline, they could see swimmers in the surf below, and colorful umbrellas on the beach. Although the bumpy ride alarmed Laura, she kept her fears to herself. From Genoa they traveled by train and bus to a village in the western Alps. From their inn they hiked over mountain trails every day. Evenings, Fermi's role as a born teacher took over. He was determined to teach his wife physics. Laura dutifully listened while he explained the Maxwell equations of electromagnetic radiation. "Therefore," he concluded his explanation, "light is nothing else but electromagnetic waves."

"I don't think so," Laura replied. "You proved only

that through some mathematical abstractions you can obtain two equal numbers."[3]

Their first motor trip together was from Rome to Laura's aunt's home in Florence—a distance of two hundred miles. They left early one morning, in a blinding rainstorm. Along the way, one tire went flat. With the spare in place, the little Peugeot chugged uphill and coasted downhill, and finally sputtered to a stop. Fermi raised the hood and found the transmission belt was worn through. Coolly, he took off his own belt and tied it around the fan. They made it to the aunt's house by nightfall. Laura was impressed by her husband's ingenuity.

Now that he had a lifetime academic appointment, Fermi set out to introduce modern physics to Italy. To do this, he planned three separate approaches: He would write articles for a wide audience, especially high school teachers; he would write a textbook on atomic physics; and he would bring promising young physicists into his department. The first goal was accomplished in the form of talks he gave at meetings of the Italian Society for the Advancement of Science, and similar occasions. These talks were then published. His textbook had been written during the summer of 1927 while Fermi vacationed in the Dolomites. Lying on his stomach in a meadow, he filled page after page, all in pencil. The handwritten pages were sent to a publisher, and the textbook came out in 1928. As for the third goal, Corbino started recruiting in order to build up the department.

Soon after Fermi started teaching in Rome in October

1926, Corbino persuaded Rasetti to come to Rome also, to fill a position that did not require a competition. Now Corbino had two good teachers in his department. But he also needed students. The best students seemed to be in the School of Engineering. Corbino succeeded in enticing a second-year engineering student named Edoardo Amaldi to switch to physics. Another engineering student, Emilio Segrè, also decided to switch. These four—Fermi, Rasetti, Amaldi, and Segrè—formed the nucleus of a team that would bring recognition and honor to their university.

Students and teachers often met in a social setting. At

LAURA AND ENRICO FERMI IN THEIR CAR IN ROME.

some of these gatherings, Fermi explained quantum theory at great length. According to quantum theory, both matter and energy can be considered as bundles of waves. This is difficult to visualize; one must accept it on faith, Fermi told the group. Since they considered Fermi infallible, and the pope is also considered to be infallible, Fermi gained the nickname "the Pope." Rasetti, who often took over when Fermi was absent, became "the Cardinal Vicar." Segrè, who often became irritable, was dubbed "Basilisk," after the mythical serpent that was said to shoot flames from its eyes when threatened. Another student, Ettore Majorana, who was a mathematical genius, became "the Great Inquisitor" because of his habit of continual questioning.[4]

The group also met periodically in Fermi's office for informal lectures and discussions. Someone might raise a question about wave mechanics, for example. This would inspire Fermi to launch into a well-thought-out explanation, as though he had carefully prepared such a lecture. Often his explanations were the development of something original. Mathematical equations filled the blackboard, and the end result was many times something worthy of publication. His application of statistical methods to high-energy physics was summarized at an international meeting in Leipzig, Germany, in 1928. This was probably the first international meeting at which Fermi took a leading part.[5]

Fermi's method of working was slow and steady. Once a method had been worked out for a particular problem, it was stored in his memory, to be brought out and applied to new problems. He could reduce a problem to simple steps. He stripped it of mathematical complications and used estimates to get at the physical application. In this way he clarified problems for his students. According to his colleague Segrè, "Whenever it was required, he was able to do elaborate mathematics; however, he first wanted to make sure that this was worth doing. He was a master at achieving important results with a minimum of effort and mathematical apparatus."[6]

Enthusiasm and morale was high within Fermi's group. The members developed long-lasting friendships. Pettiness or jealousy never arose. However, outside of their group, politics came into play. As with most university faculties, professors jostled for bigger budgets, larger departments, or more influence. A certain professor of advanced physics, jealously guarding his domain in the department, opposed Corbino's establishment of new professorships. In addition, this "Mr. North," as he was nicknamed, kept his own assistants in the dark about the goals of research projects he supervised. It was rumored in the physics building that his mere presence jinxed experiments. Hydrogen tubes would explode mysteriously as "Mr. North" predicted.[7]

Corbino wanted to propose Fermi for membership in the Accademia dei Lincei, a prestigious organization. He could not do it himself because he was to be out of the country at the time of their meeting. He asked "Mr. North" to read his letter of nomination at the meeting.

Upon Corbino's return, he found out that Fermi was still not a member. The professor had conveniently forgotten to read the letter.

Soon it was Corbino's turn to get even. Mussolini distrusted the Accademia dei Lincei because he believed that its members were hostile to Fascism. He decided to form a rival group, the Accademia d'Italia, or Royal Academy of Italy, which was to "promote, help with advice and financial support, coordinate and channel the intellectual work . . . of the nation."[8] The first thirty persons were to be named in March 1929. "North" had high

EMILIO SEGRÈ, ENRICO PERSICO, AND ENRICO FERMI (LEFT TO RIGHT) ENJOY A DAY AT THE BEACH.

hopes that he would be among them. Imagine how he felt when he found out the only physicist among the appointees was Fermi, who did not even have ties to the Fascist party!

The Accademia d'Italia gave its members an additional salary, a fancy uniform, and the title of "Excellency." Fermi appreciated being the only physicist elected. It was a great honor for someone only twenty-seven years old. But he did not care for the other accompaniments. The main advantage to him was the generous salary that went with the appointment. It gave him a great sense of security. The title of His Excellency caused him embarrassment, as did the flashy uniform and sword he was required to purchase and wear at his inauguration. He was a striking sight as he drove off in his little yellow car, wearing a heavily embroidered vest, feathered hat, and black cloak.

Members of the Accademia were supposed to attend occasional government-sponsored events. On one such evening, Fermi decided to go work in his lab instead. But a street he needed to cross was blocked off by police. He showed his official invitation, and told the policemen, "I am the driver for His Excellency Professor Fermi. I am on my way to pick him up. He would be extremely angry if you do not let me through." He was immediately allowed to pass.

Fermi's physicists needed to learn more experimental techniques. For this purpose, they scattered to work in other laboratories. Rasetti went to Pasadena, California;

Segrè went to Amsterdam; Amaldi to Leipzig. Rasetti then moved on to Berlin, and Segrè to Hamburg. Eventually they all returned to Rome.

Corbino continued to enlarge his department. He pulled strings to have a vacancy on the science faculty diverted to physics, and got Rasetti to fill it as a professor of spectroscopy. Segrè then moved into Rasetti's position, Amaldi moved into Segrè's, and thus another opening was produced. Because of the political situation in Germany in the early 1930s and the growing reputation of the Roman group, young German physicists came to Rome. Some stayed, while others went on to the United States. The resulting interchange of scientific ideas was profitable for all concerned.

In the summer of 1930 Fermi was invited to teach at the University of Michigan. His lectures in English were filled with mispronounced words, for his knowledge of English came from reading scientific journals and books by Jack London. Two scientist friends agreed to listen to his lectures and point out mispronounced or misused words. By the end of the summer, his mistakes were down to one or two; those that remained made his classes interesting and fun, according to the two friends.[9]

While in the United States, the Fermis were often asked what they thought of Mussolini. Fascism by this time was looked upon with tolerance in Italy and elsewhere. Italian citizens hardly noticed that their freedom was being progressively restricted, while all powers were being concentrated in the person of Mussolini. The

Fermis gave noncommital answers to their questioners. The other common question, "How do you like America?", they could answer more enthusiastically. Who could not like a country where everyone was kind and hospitable? Besides the well-equipped laboratories and the friendly atmosphere among scientists, Fermi was attracted to the political ideals of America. The idea of emigration returned, stronger than before.

In the summers of 1933, 1935, 1936, and 1937 Fermi returned to the University of Michigan. Gradually he was becoming Americanized. After each trip he talked about permanently moving to the U.S., though his wife, Laura, remained reluctant to leave their native Italy.

CHAPTER FIVE

EXPERIMENTS ON ATOMIC NUCLEI

With the general acceptance of quantum theory, most physicists believed that everything about atomic behavior was known. Future research, they thought, lay in the exploration of the atomic nucleus. In a speech given in September 1929, Corbino stated that to achieve a modification of the atomic nucleus, "the only way that remains is artificially to produce projectiles similar to those of radioactive bodies but in much greater quantity and with greater velocity."[1]

The British physicist Ernest Rutherford had discovered that alpha particles given off by a radioactive element are positively charged atoms of helium—that is, they are helium nuclei. Beta particles are actually electrons. These discoveries led to many experiments to make other elements radioactive. This was done by shooting alpha particles at a thin layer of the element being investigated.

The French physicists Frédéric Joliot and his wife Irène (who was the daughter of the two-time Nobelist Marie Curie) found that when light elements such as beryllium were bombarded with alpha particles, electrically neutral particles were released. The English physicist James Chadwick, working in Rutherford's laboratory, showed in 1932 that these neutral particles had a mass close to that of a proton. They were given the name neutrons. The positive charge of an atom was shown to be concentrated in a tiny nucleus, but the nucleus also contains neutrons. Surrounding the nucleus are the negatively charged electrons. We can imagine the structure as an extremely tiny solar system, in which the nucleus represents the sun and the electrons represent the planets.

Rutherford in 1919 was the first to show that some bombardments resulted in a different element. When he used nitrogen as his target, each nitrogen nucleus was transformed into oxygen (its neighbor on the periodic chart).[2] The Joliots discovered other bombardments that created this result. For example, boron became nitrogen; magnesium produced a mixture of silicon and aluminum. Through the capture of an alpha particle and subsequent emission of a proton, aluminum became silicon. Sometimes the product of such artificial radioactivity is an element slightly different from the naturally-occurring form of that element. Its nucleus may have one or two or three more neutrons than the naturally-occurring one, or it may have fewer neutrons. Such varieties of an element are called isotopes. Bombardment of nitrogen produces oxygen, but it is an isotope containing nine neutrons rather than the eight in naturally-occurring oxygen. The number of protons in isotopes, however, is always the same; they are equal to the number of electrons in an electrically neutral atom of the element.

Physicists calculated the energy going into a nucleus under bombardment, and the energy given off. They found that a small amount of energy was unaccounted for. Where did it go? Wolfgang Pauli had already proposed that a new particle, practically undetectable, carried off the missing energy. Fermi gave this new particle the name neutrino, meaning little neutral one.

It was found that in certain radioactive elements, a strange transformation takes place. The neutrons in the nucleus break down, or decay, leaving in each case a proton, an electron, and a neutrino. The electrons move quickly away, producing a stream of beta rays. Each atom left behind now has one less neutron and one more proton. Because the atom has a positive charge, it can attract a free electron and again become neutral in its charge. But because it now has an extra proton, it has become a different element.

In 1933 Fermi wrote a paper using mathematics to describe the above process, called beta-decay. He introduced a new type of force called the "weak force" to calculate the probability of this transformation and the distribution of energy among the electrons taking part in beta-decay.[3] A new fundamental constant was needed to make the math come out right. This constant, now called the Fermi constant, was determined from experimental data. The weak force became one of the four fundamental forces in physics; the others are gravity, electromagnetic force, and the strong force (which holds an atomic nucleus together).

Fermi's paper on beta-decay was of fundamental importance for the later development of nuclear physics. But the English scientific journal *Nature* refused to publish it, claiming it was too abstract and speculative. It was finally published in an Italian journal, and soon after, in a German one.

After studying the results reported by the Joliots of alpha-particle bombardment, Fermi realized that alpha particles do not make good projectiles with which to study radioactivity. Since they carry a positive charge, the negatively charged electrons of the target atoms slow them down greatly. Those that do come in contact with a nucleus are immediately driven off by the likewise positively charged nucleus. So Fermi decided to use neutrons to shoot at various elements rather than alpha particles. Neutrons, being small and neutral, would not bounce off like the heavier, positively charged alpha particles.

Until then, Fermi had been a theoretical physicist. After his work on beta-decay, he was ready to tackle something different, as a change of pace. He would become an experimentalist. But for that purpose he had to learn new techniques. Rasetti was expert at building

ENRICO FERMI RELAXES ON THE DECK OF A SHIP DURING A TRIP BY SEA, CIRCA 1938.

equipment, and would no doubt have helped, but he was in Morocco for a long vacation. The first thing Fermi needed was a Geiger counter to detect products of radioactivity. Though common today, in 1934 Geiger counters were still a novelty. Fermi set to work to build one himself, and soon had a workable model.

Next he needed a source of neutrons. For this, he used the same procedure Chadwick had employed in first discovering the neutron: bombarding the element beryllium with alpha particles. But where would the alpha particles come from? For that, Fermi turned to Professor Trabacchi, director of the physics laboratory of the

Bureau of Public Health, which was located in the university's physics building. Trabacchi, with admirable foresight, kept a gram of radium in his lab. Radium breaks down naturally into the gas radon, which in turn emits alpha particles.

Trabacchi made the radon available to Fermi, as well as the apparatus to separate radon from radium. To produce the needed neutrons, Fermi or his coworkers mixed beryllium powder with radon. When an occasional beryllium nucleus is hit by an alpha particle, the beryllium is changed into carbon—a slightly heavier element—and one neutron is released. This neutron is now free to hit nuclei of other elements present.

An orderly series of experiments was planned. First neutrons would be shot at hydrogen, the lightest element, then helium, the next lightest, then lithium, and so on, through successively heavier elements. The first experiments were disappointing; nothing had happened. Fermi got discouraged, but his stubbornness would not let him quit. He continued with other elements. At last, with fluorine, he got results. Fluorine was strongly activated with neutrons. Encouraged, Fermi put Segrè and Amaldi to work on the project, and sent a cable to Rasetti in Morocco, asking him to return immediately.

Segrè was put in charge of obtaining the rarer elements, because of his flair for business. The main supplier of chemicals in Rome was very helpful. He even gave Segrè free samples of two soft metals, cesium and rubidium, saying, "They have been in my store for the last fifteen years and nobody has ever asked for them."[4]

The apparatus to extract radon consisted of a glass tube several feet tall, attached at one end to the container of radium and at the other end to a purifying unit. The radon gas was collected in a half-inch-long glass tube, which was cooled to turn it into a liquid. Then the tube had to be sealed by a gas flame. The first few times they tried this, the tube broke. Then they found a way to seal the tubes without breaking them. Fresh radon was extracted once a week. Geiger counters to measure the radioactivity were at the other end of a long corridor. Fermi and Amaldi would race down the hall with their sample, because sometimes the radioactivity faded away after a minute, or less.

After producing an activated substance, the researchers next had to determine what it was. That meant they had to separate the active portion from the rest. But ordinary chemical methods would not work because the quantities were so small. Fortunately, a method was found. If the radioactive atoms of an element are mixed with nonradioactive amounts of the same element, they can be separated. All one needs to do is guess what element the original one had turned into through its bombardment.

For example, when iron was bombarded with neutrons, some of it became radioactive and turned into another element that is close to iron in the periodic chart. Consequently the researchers dissolved the activated iron in nitric acid and added small quantities of cobalt, chromium, and manganese. These could be separated by ordinary chemical methods. Each portion was then tested with a Geiger counter. The portion with manganese registered radioactivity. Therefore the physicists concluded that the iron had turned into manganese.

Fermi had been a theoretical physicist. After his work on beta-decay, he would become an experimentalist.

These experiments led to a whole series of publications. Even before actual publication, new developments were communicated to about forty prominent physicists around the world. Rutherford sent a handwritten note congratulating Fermi on his interesting new experiments. Fermi's reputation, which had already been strong, grew even stronger.

When Fermi and his group had worked their way through the periodic chart, they finally came to uranium, the heaviest element. They found that bombardment of uranium with neutrons produced more than one element. One of these seemed to be an element of atomic number 93, which does not exist naturally. They announced their results in the journal Ricerca Scientifica in May 1934. Rather than claiming that a new element had been produced, they simply stated that they had indications that such an element might have been formed. But Corbino, in a speech to the Accademia dei Lincei in June, stated proudly that "I feel I can conclude that production of this (new) element has already been definitely ascertained."[5]

The Fascist press jumped on this bit of news. Italian

newspapers crowed about how the contribution of these scientists "proves once more how in the Fascist atmosphere Italy has resumed her ancient role of teacher and vanguard in all fields."[6] Leading foreign newspapers also ran the sensational story, although some added that scientists were not willing to accept Corbino's announcement until details of Fermi's work were published.

Fermi was terribly upset. He wished Corbino had not mentioned anything about element 93. He had always hated publicity, but now he also felt his reputation was at stake. He decided that he and Corbino would prepare a statement for the press. The statement they released said, in part:

"The public is giving an incorrect interpretation . . . to Senator Corbino's speech. . . . It has been ascertained in my researches that . . . many elements bombarded with neutrons change into different elements having radioactive properties. . . . Because uranium is the last of the elements in the atomic series, it appears possible that the element produced should be the following, namely, 93. . . . Numerous and delicate tests must still be performed before production of element 93 is actually proved. . . . At any rate the principal purpose of this research is not to produce a new element, but to study the general phenomenon."[7]

The experiments were going well in the first half of 1934, but Fermi had to interrupt his work for the summer. He had agreed to deliver lectures in Argentina and Brazil. In Buenos Aires he and his wife were treated like royalty. They stayed in an elegant hotel, and the Argentines vied with one another to offer lavish meals and entertainment.

That fall, a young physicist, Bruno Pontecorvo, joined Fermi's group. He and Amaldi got some strange results in their radioactivity experiments. The test materials were shaped into a hollow cylinder, and the neutron source was placed inside it. The cylinder then was placed inside a lead box to shield it from outside radiation. In the case of silver, the cylinder gave differing results, depending on how far away it was placed from the sides of the lead box. Outside of the box, the radioactivity was greater when the apparatus was placed on a wooden table rather than one of metal or stone.

In an effort to explain the action of the surrounding lead, a lead wedge was prepared, to be placed between the neutron source and the detector. As Fermi explained later "I took great pains to have the piece of lead precisely machined. I was clearly dissatisfied with something; I tried every excuse to postpone putting the piece of lead in its place. When finally, with some reluctance, I was going to put it in its place, I said to myself 'No, I do not want this piece of lead here; what I want is a piece of paraffin.' It was just like that, with no advance warning, no conscious prior reasoning."[8]

The researchers put the neutron source inside a big block of paraffin, irradiated the silver cylinder, and measured its radioactivity. The Geiger counter went crazy! The radioactivity of silver increased up to one hundred times! Everybody was called in to watch the miraculous effect of paraffin. A few other materials were tried, but none had the same effect. What had happened?

During their long lunch hour, Fermi tried to explain this puzzle. Paraffin contains lots of hydrogen atoms, and hydrogen nuclei are about the same size as neutrons. Neutrons, he reasoned, must have hit hydrogen nuclei and lost some of their energy in the collision. These slowed-down neutrons had more of a chance of being captured by the silver nuclei. So the conclusion was that slow neutrons are better at producing radioactivity than fast ones.

Would other substances containing a large proportion of hydrogen give the same results? Water seemed a promising substance, and it is readily available. Behind the physics building was a fountain containing goldfish. This area was the private garden of the Corbino family, who lived on the top floor of the physics building. It was a handy place to test Fermi's theory. The scientists rushed their neutron source and silver cylinder to the fountain. It worked! So water also increased the radioactivity of silver![9]

That evening, the entire group of researchers gathered at the Amaldis' home to write a report to the Ricerca Scientifica. They were eager to publish their finding, but when Corbino was told about it, he became upset.

"Can't you see that your discovery may have industrial applications? You should take out a patent before you give out more details," Corbino told them.[10] The men had not thought about that. Scientists usually did not take out patents on their discoveries. Anyway, the amounts of radioactive elements had been too small to consider any practical applications. But Corbino insisted, and so a few days later, Fermi and his six assistants applied for a patent. Just a few years later, this patent became very important to the U.S. government.

By the end of 1934, Fermi's team had published twenty-five different papers dealing with neutrons. The pace of research then slowed down. In the fall of 1935, Fermi's group fell apart. Rasetti was in the U.S. for a year, Segrè took a position in Palermo on the island of Sicily, and Pontecorvo left for France.

Fermi and Amaldi continued their neutron experiments, and Fermi worked on the theory of the slowing-down process. They began each workday at eight, and continued with almost no breaks until six or seven in the evening. There was no time for seminars or private lectures for students. Fermi became more reserved. While he could always communicate with ease, he had never readily confided his innermost thoughts to anyone, and now he was even less likely to do so. His research took up all of his time and his energy.

CHAPTER SIX

MOMENTOUS CHANGES

Italy went to war in Ethiopia in October 1935. The mood of the entire Italian population was somber. Everyone was worried about the changes the war could bring—a political crisis or a revolt caused by the unstable economy.

Meanwhile, German-Jewish scientists who were dismissed from their posts emigrated to other countries. Their considerable contributions to physics were discredited and rejected as "Jewish physics." Many Italian physicists tried to help their dismissed German friends, but there was not much they could do. Italy was slipping further and further under the influence of Germany. The alliance of the two countries was given formal status in November 1936.

In March 1938, the German army marched into Austria and declared it part of a Greater Germany. At first Mussolini was undecided what his reaction should be.

Italian newspapers and radio broadcasts withheld their comments until they were given some directives from the government. In the end, Mussolini praised the "statesmanship" of the German dictator Adolf Hitler.[1]

The following May, Italy made gala preparations for a visit by Hitler. Peasant houses along his travel route were repainted, and Fascist slogans were posted, proclaiming in large letters "Mussolini is always right" and "To win is necessary, but to fight is more necessary."[2]

In July 1938, the Italian government began passing racial laws similar to Germany's. A document issued by the government stated that "Jews do not belong to the Italian race." They were stripped of their citizenship rights. Many Jewish-owned firms were broken up. Non-Jews were not allowed to work for Jews or live in their homes. Later, Jewish children were excluded from public schools, and Jewish teachers were dismissed. Another law forbade marriage between Jews and non-Jews. Other laws were passed in rapid succession, some on trivial issues such as clothing. It seemed as if the government wanted to show its power by regulating all aspects of daily life.[3] To make this anti-Semitism respectable, the government tried to get scientists to sign a statement of agreement. Most of them, to their credit, refused.

Fermi looked on the Fascist slogans with distaste. He had never reconciled himself to the aims of the Fascist government. Now the racial laws brought on feelings of alarm and foreboding. It was not clear what could happen to Fermi's wife and children. Fermi made up his mind to leave Italy at the earliest opportunity. That opportunity would come soon.

Professor Corbino had died in January 1937. This was a blow to Fermi's group because Corbino had given them much guidance and encouragement. Corbino's successor was the unpopular professor, "Mr. North," who had opposed Fermi's election to the Accademia dei Lincei. The physics department moved from the old building to new, larger quarters on the university's main campus. This meant that all work had to stop until the move was completed.

Before moving, Fermi, Amaldi, and Rasetti built a small accelerator to replace the radon/beryllium source of neutrons. In an accelerator charged particles are whirled around a circle, gaining more energy with each revolution by means of a strong magnetic field. At a pre-determined energy level, the particles are slammed into a target.

In the fall of 1938, at a physics meeting in Copenhagen, the Danish physicist Niels Bohr mentioned to Fermi that his name was on the list of candidates for the Nobel Prize. Fermi was told in advance because the committee wanted to be sure that the Italian government would not prevent him from accepting the award, if indeed he was the winner. In the past, the governments of Germany and Italy had prevented some prize-winners from accepting their awards. Fermi assured Bohr that he would be free to accept.

The Fermis' phone rang early in the morning of November 10, 1938. An unfamiliar voice asked Laura,

"Is this Professor Fermi's residence?" Upon being told it was, the caller continued: "I wish to inform you that this evening at six Professor Fermi will be called on the telephone from Stockholm."

Laura, in great excitement, ran to the bedroom. "Wake up, Enrico! This evening you will be called on the telephone from Stockholm!"

Fermi, now fully awake, propped himself up on an elbow. "It must mean the Nobel Prize!" He paused. "So the possibilities that were hinted to me have become true, and it was right to make our plans as we did."[4]

Laura's excitement drained away as she realized that the often-discussed plans to emigrate were now about to come true. The thought of leaving Rome filled her with dread. Her family and friends were there. Her whole life was bound up with Rome. Earlier that year they had moved into a larger apartment that had a bathroom lined with beautiful green marble. They had servants' quarters for a cook and a maid. Fascism so far had not interfered with their lives. Scientists and scholars were far removed from politics; in fact, they were respected, even revered. What lay in store for the Fermi family? How would being transplanted to another country affect them?

The Fermis celebrated the news by going on a shopping spree. They both got new watches. Laura drank in the sights of Rome—the many fountains, the charming old buildings—knowing that soon they would be only fond memories.

The awaited phone call came shortly after six in the

evening. The citation, read over the phone, stated "To Professor Fermi of Rome for his identification of new radioactive elements produced by neutron bombardment and his discovery, made in connection with this work, of nuclear reactions effected by slow neutrons." He was to be the sole recipient in the field of physics. Often the prize went to two or three individuals who would share the prize money. But Fermi would not have to share it with anyone. The four years of hard work had paid off amazingly well.

Shortly after the phone call, a group of the family's friends crowded into their home. Amaldi's wife Ginestra took charge of the household. The cook was instructed to prepare a banquet. The maid was told to set a long table. Wine was brought out, and the group celebrated Fermi's award.[5]

As soon as he made the final decision to emigrate, Fermi had written to four American universities. He asked if their former offers of teaching positions were still open; if so, he could now accept. The letters were mailed from four different towns so as not to arouse the suspicion of Italian authorities. The Fermis' passports could have been withdrawn if their plans were to become known. If anyone connected with the government had asked, Fermi would say he was going abroad for only six or seven months. Since he had traveled so often abroad to lecture at foreign universities, the government would probably regard the trip as routine.[6] Now, of course, there was a valid reason to leave the country: to go to

Stockholm. No one other than Rasetti and the Amaldis knew that the Fermis would not return.

Enrico and Laura, their two children, and the children's nanny left Rome by train on December 6, 1938. Rasetti and the Amaldis came to the station to see them off. The two co-workers were saddened that their research group was breaking up for good. Although Rasetti and Segrè had each spent time at other universities, the nucleus of the group had up to that time remained in Rome. Segrè had also decided not to return to Italy, after teaching the past summer at the University of California at Berkeley. Rasetti was looking for a position abroad, and would leave the following summer for Laval University in Canada. That would leave only Amaldi of the original group.

As they waited for the train, Ginestra Amaldi reproached the Fermis: "Enrico's departure is a betrayal of the young people who have come to study with him and who have trusted in him for guidance and help."[7] Her husband objected to her statement. It is Fascism that should be blamed, he said, not Fermi. Laura's doubts surfaced again. Which of one's obligations should come first? To one's country or one's children? To one's family or one's students? Her emotions were in a whirl as the conductor shouted "All aboard!" and they settled into their seats.

The question had arisen whether the children's nanny could come along on their trip. Fermi had talked to the American consul in Rome, who was not encouraging.

The Italian authorities wanted to make sure the nanny would return to Italy. She produced a fiancé—a guarantee that she would return—and the visa was granted. The words "Nobel Prize" mentioned to the authorities also hastened the issuing of her visa.[8]

Laura drank in the sights of Rome— knowing that soon they would be only fond memories.

The Fermis were tense and worried that something would happen at the country's borders to upset their plans. At the German border, a guard entered the train to inspect passports. He turned the pages of the Fermis' passports over and over. Tension mounted as the inspection dragged on. Fermi spoke to the guard in German: Was something wrong? The guard apparently could not find the stamped page showing a visa from the German consulate, which indicated permission to enter the country. Fermi pointed out the place, and the guard smiled as he handed back the passports. A burden was lifted from their minds.

After traveling for forty-eight hours, the family arrived in Stockholm. Everyone put on warm clothing for protection in the northern climate. Almost immediately the family was drawn into the festivities associated with the awards.

On December 10, the anniversary of Alfred Nobel's death, the Stockholm Concert Hall was filled to capacity, with everyone in formal wear. That day the prizes in physics and literature were the only ones awarded. The literature prize went to Pearl S. Buck, the American writer of novels set in China. She and Fermi sat in tall armchairs on the stage, while members of the Swedish Academy and past recipients of Nobel Prizes were seated behind them. The king of Sweden, Gustav V, sat in the first row facing the stage.

The presentation speech for the prize in physics was given by Professor H. Pleijel, chairman of the committee that chose the recipient for physics. He related the history of discoveries dealing with radioactivity and the structure of atomic nuclei. He ended his speech this way:

> Professor Fermi, the Royal Academy of Science of Sweden has awarded you the Nobel Prize for Physics in 1938 for your discovery of new radioactive substances belonging to the entire range of elements and for the discovery you made in the course of this work of the selective power of slow neutrons. We offer our congratulations and express the highest admiration for your brilliant researches, which throw new light on the constitution of atomic nuclei and open up new horizons for the further development of atomic investigation. I beg you now to receive the Nobel Prize from the hands of His Majesty the King.

Fermi rose and came down the four steps to receive the medal, a diploma, and an envelope from the king. Because it was the custom never to turn one's back on royalty, he then retreated backward and sank into his chair. Later he would brag about having done this without stumbling or faltering. The fact that he shook hands with the king was severely criticized in the Italian press. He was expected instead to give the stiff-armed Fascist salute. But this was something Fermi would never do.

FERMI RECEIVES HIS NOBEL PRIZE FROM KING GUSTAV V OF SWEDEN ON DECEMBER 10, 1938.

The Italian newspapers gave the entire ceremony only a three-line announcement. The press was uncertain, perhaps even fearful, how Italy's ally Germany would react to an Italian accepting the Nobel Prize. Germany had forbidden one of its citizens, Carl von Ossietzky, from accepting the peace prize in 1935, and also any future German recipients.[9] The Italian ambassador to Sweden, however, remained very hospitable to the Fermis.

A dinner with the king at his palace followed the ceremony. King Gustav V had a poor appetite. This proved unfortunate for the dinner guests, because as soon as the king laid down his fork, waiters whisked away everybody's plates. This was repeated with each course that was served.[10]

Between the time of the Nobel awards and the publication of Fermi's acceptance speech, new discoveries were made in Germany. Otto Hahn and Fritz Strassmann had produced radioactive barium among the products of neutron bombardment of uranium. This was interpreted by the Austrian physicist Lise Meitner as proof that the uranium nucleus had split into two fragments. This splitting is called fission, and is accompanied by the release of great amounts of energy.

News of this discovery was flashed throughout the scientific world. Although Fermi's group had not forseen the possibility of the nucleus splitting when conducting their experiments, the discovery of fission was certainly hastened by their work. In the coming years, Fermi would be a trailblazer in putting the discovery of nuclear fission to practical use.

However, Fermi was unaware of these new discoveries during his last days in Europe. From Stockholm the family went to Copenhagen, where they spent a few days with Niels Bohr. Then they sailed to England, and on December 24 they boarded the *Franconia*. As the New York skyline came into view on January 2, 1939, Fermi turned to his wife with a smile and announced, "We have founded the American branch of the Fermi family."

THE WAR
EFFORT

From among the teaching offers Fermi received, he accepted the one from Columbia University in New York. He began teaching the standard physics courses, and transferred his usual enthusiasm for the subject to his students. In addition, he taught a course in geophysics, using the principles of physics to explain the earth's composition and the physical changes it has undergone.[1] He tried earnestly to assimilate American culture and to improve his spoken English. In this respect he was helped by George B. Pegram, head of the physics department at Columbia.

Fermi found out about the German fission experiments shortly after his arrival. Niels Bohr came to the United States for a conference on theoretical physics, and the two discussed the phenomenon of fission and its significance. Most physicists realized that if uranium splits into two parts, each fragment will have more neutrons than a stable nucleus of the resulting element. The nucleus must release excess neutrons in order to become stable again. These released neutrons can then go on to split other uranium nuclei. This would lead to a chain reaction. But could such a reaction be achieved in the laboratory?

The concept of a chain reaction had occurred to a Hungarian physicist named Leo Szilard before it had actually been discovered. Szilard had studied in Germany, moved to England, and later, to the U.S. He was living in New York when Fermi arrived, and often visited the physicists at Columbia. He had no teaching position because he did not like university routines. He preferred to work alone, often in an erratic manner. Besides physics, he was interested in biology and economics, and he enjoyed meeting politicians and businessmen. He associated with other Hungarian scientists who were then in the U.S. and who were interested in world politics.[2]

Szilard realized that fission had enormous potential if it could be harnessed. Its explosive power could dwarf any conventional bomb. Therefore it was extremely important that the technology leading to a chain reaction not fall into the wrong hands. He urged American scientists to carefully guard scientific information on fission.

Europe in 1939 was drifting into war. After annexing Austria in 1938, Hitler took over parts of Czechoslovakia later that same year. It became evident that he intended to create a Greater Germany by swallowing up neighboring countries. Scientists who had fled from Germany realized the danger.

Szilard communicated his worries about fission technology to Pegram at Columbia. Fermi agreed with Pegram that the U.S. government should be alerted. In March 1939 Pegram wrote a letter to the Chief of Naval Operations asking for a way to transfer results of the work done at Columbia to the proper authorities in the U.S. Navy. As a result of this letter, Fermi spoke to a group at the Navy Department, and the Navy allocated a small sum to support the physicists' research.

While Fermi spent the summer of 1939 in Ann Arbor, Michigan, Szilard was still worried and impatient. He approached Albert Einstein, who was then at his summer home on Long Island. Szilard asked him to write a letter to President Roosevelt. Because of Einstein's worldwide reputation, Szilard believed a letter from Einstein would carry more weight than a letter from anyone else.

Einstein's letter, dated August 2, 1939, explained that uranium may be an important source of energy, and that a nuclear chain reaction could lead to an extremely powerful bomb. Einstein recommended that a contact person be appointed to keep the government informed of the physicists' work. The letter was not actually hand-delivered to the President until October 11, however.[3] By this time, World War II had already started in Europe.

President Roosevelt realized the urgency of the situation. He set up an Advisory Committee, which received a $6,000 grant from the Army and Navy. Later, a larger amount—$140,000—was obtained. A National Defense Research Committee was set up to help science become part of the war effort.

Fermi was only interested in fission as a natural phenomenon—as a process that would help to gain insights into the workings of atomic nuclei. Since much of his equipment had been left in Rome, he turned again to theoretical studies. With all his traveling, he had fallen behind in reading the scientific literature. He spent his time catching up with what had been published. Fortunately he could digest quickly whatever he read. He would read the writer's statement of the problem, then scribble some calculations, and finally compare the writer's solution with his own.[4]

At Columbia Fermi got the opportunity to work with the university's circular accelerator, called a cyclotron. He turned into an experimentalist again. The cyclotron was able to produce 100,000 more neutrons per second than the radon/beryllium source in Rome. Fermi could not resist such a challenge.

The study of a nuclear chain reaction was taken up by many physicists around the world. In the U.S., it was mostly refugee scientists from Europe who worked on this project. American scientists were working on the development of radar, which was considered more important in the war-time atmosphere of 1939 and 1940.[5] Europeans were still considered aliens, not eligible to work on secret projects. But they were the ones who were alert to the possibilities of new weapons from uranium, and to the danger posed by the Nazi government of Germany. Most were not convinced that an atomic bomb was possible, but they still felt it should be studied.

In 1941 American and English scientists also became interested in atomic energy. England and Germany were at war. Perhaps Germany was working on developing an atomic bomb—but there was no way to find out. Reluctantly, Fermi was drawn into the work that would in time produce the atomic bomb.

Fermi, as the greatest living expert on neutrons, led a group at Columbia who concentrated their efforts on getting quantitative information on the secondary neutrons formed in fission. Not all of the neutrons emitted during fission will go on to split more uranium atoms. Many are absorbed before they have a chance to hit uranium nuclei. The neutrons are too fast, and not effective, unless they are slowed down.

Fermi was perfectly suited for this work because of his combination of experimental and theoretical talents. Often he could predict the outcome of an experiment. Measurements and calculations usually confirmed his predictions. His ability and scientific judgment were widely admired by all, and he inspired immense confidence in all who worked with him. Like an orchestra conductor who draws a fine performance out of his musicians, Fermi could lead his coworkers to excellence.[6]

A major problem was to determine how many neutrons

Fission

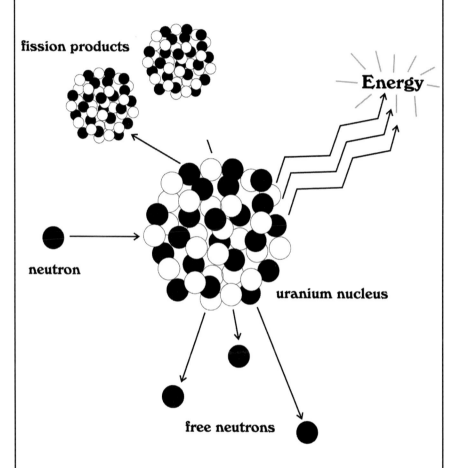

fission products

Energy

neutron

uranium nucleus

free neutrons

WHEN A NEUTRON SPLITS THE NUCLEUS OF A U-235 ATOM, TWO SMALLER FRAGMENTS RESULT, ALONG WITH FREE NEUTRONS AND A TREMENDOUS AMOUNT OF ENERGY. THE FREE NEUTRONS GO ON TO SPLIT THE NUCLEI OF OTHER ATOMS OF THE URANIUM IN A CHAIN REACTION.

were emitted by each uranium atom for each neutron that it absorbed. This was affected by the very brief formation of an unstable particle, a phenomenon known as resonance absorption. Fermi came up with a rough estimate of this effect. He concluded that lumping uranium rather than mixing it uniformly with the medium substance would reduce the losses due to resonance absorption. Fermi's intuition proved correct again. He also realized that water absorbed too many neutrons and was therefore not suitable as a medium for a chain reaction. Upon Szilard's recommendation, he introduced the use of graphite (a form of carbon, also used in pencil lead) as a moderator to slow down the neutrons.[7] A formula was developed that linked mathematically the propagation of neutrons to the various factors affecting it.[8]

Like an orchestra conductor who draws a fine performance out of his musicians, Fermi could lead his coworkers to excellence.

Uranium occurs naturally in two isotope forms: uranium-238, which has 92 protons and 146 neutrons in the nucleus, and uranium-235, with 92 protons and 143 neutrons. The form that can undergo fission is uranium-235, but this isotope constitutes only 0.7% of natural uranium. Separating it is very difficult. The separation was eventually accomplished with the help of the staff of industrial companies.

An alternative method was possible that did not involve isotope separation. Lise Meitner had shown that uranium-238 could capture neutrons and then emit an electron. This product was identified as element 93, later given the name neptunium. This neptunium, also radioactive, releases an electron (another example of beta-decay) and becomes element 94, with a mass of 239, later called plutonium. It seemed probable that plutonium would undergo fission when bombarded with slow neutrons.[9] A chain reaction with natural-occurring uranium produced by fast neutrons would lead to formation of a certain amount of plutonium. If this could be separated, it could be used to build a bomb.

When Emilio Segrè came from California to visit Fermi in December 1940, they discussed this topic at great length. Fermi asked Segrè to undertake an investigation of plutonium at his laboratory on the Berkeley campus. Berkeley had a new sixty-inch cyclotron which produced high-energy neutrons. Segrè's group succeeded in separating the neptunium and plutonium formed by neutron bombardment of uranium. They showed that plutonium-239 was potential bomb material. So now there were two paths to build a bomb. Segrè communicated his results to Fermi, but could do so only through another person, because they were both aliens and were not supposed to communicate directly.

In December 1941 Japan attacked the United States at Pearl Harbor, and the U.S. entered the war. Now the uranium program took on more urgency. Arthur H. Compton of the University of Chicago was put in charge of the scientific work. He decided to bring all the work to Chicago. His group was to be called the Metallurgical Laboratory.

During 1941, Fermi and Szilard in New York had begun building an atomic reactor, or "pile," in which layers of graphite alternated with graphite containing chunks of uranium. Getting enough of each material was a problem. Szilard used his contacts, and soon tons of pure graphite began arriving at the physics building. Fermi's pile eventually reached the ceiling, but it still was not large enough for a chain reaction. Not enough neutrons were available to produce fission. While the group was looking for a larger room, they got word that they would be moving to Chicago.

Fermi was still an Italian citizen. Now that the U.S. was at war with Japan, Germany, and Italy, he was considered an enemy alien. Aliens were not allowed on airplanes. They could not own cameras or short-wave radios. Before any trip, they had to let a district attorney know at least seven days before leaving their community.[10]

Fermi had to travel to Chicago often. But in order to get the required permit to travel, he had to plan his trips ten days in advance. At first he was good-natured about these rules. But one time, the permit did not arrive in time. A secretary had to be sent to pick it up in person. This disturbed Fermi greatly. He grumbled, "If they want me to travel for them, they'll have to find a way to let me do so freely."[11] Eventually the U.S. government did relax its rules.

The group from Columbia moved to Chicago in

ONE OF THE MANY EXPERIMENTAL PILES MADE AT THE UNIVERSITY OF CHICAGO.

stages. Fermi was not happy about having to move. He liked working with a small group, where he could keep track of everything going on. In Chicago he felt his group would be swallowed up in the huge organization of the Metallurgical Laboratory. In April 1942 he moved to Chicago permanently, while his family remained in the East to let the children finish the school year.

In the meantime, the Fermis were fearful their loyalty would be questioned. They burned one of their children's books that showed many pictures of Mussolini. Their five-year-old son, Giulio, caused alarm by going around the neighborhood saying he wished Hitler and Mussolini would win the war. His father scolded him severely. The boy sobbed, "I didn't mean it!", and the incident was soon forgotten.[12]

In Chicago Fermi found himself attending endless meetings. Instead of performing experiments, he had others do them. All he could do himself was analyze their data, and give advice when asked. Another source of annoyance was the censoring of his mail. He complained angrily, and the censorship stopped.

In mid-1942 it was still unknown which method was best to prepare material for fission. The uranium project spread out to many universities and industries. The urgency of the war made it necessary to divide up the work. Everything had to be done in secret. This was hard on the scientists, who were used to exchanging information. With the appointment of General Leslie R. Groves, the whole undertaking was put under military control. Groves knew how to organize and coordinate many tasks, and he got along well with the scientists.

Upon General Groves' orders, land was purchased at Argonne, near Chicago, for the expanded work of the Metallurgical Laboratory. Land was also acquired at three additional sites: Oak Ridge in Tennessee, Los Alamos in New Mexico, and Hanford in the state of Washington. Construction began at Argonne, but a labor union strike soon brought it to a halt. Fermi then proposed that the reactor be built under Stagg Field, the University of

Chicago's stadium.[13] The location in the heart of the city worried Groves and Compton, but they gave their consent.

Football had been suspended at the Chicago campus, so Stagg Field was being used for other purposes. Underneath the west stands was a squash court, thirty feet wide, sixty feet long, and more than twenty-six feet high. The physicists had hoped to have more space, but this was all they could get. Crates began arriving from New York, as graphite and uranium from Columbia were shipped to Chicago, along with Geiger counters and other instruments.

Fermi was now given a bodyguard, a six-foot two-hundred-pound man named John Baudino. Fermi was too valuable to risk any harm coming to him. Baudino was supposed to drive Fermi to Argonne whenever he was needed there. But Fermi's independent spirit would not allow anyone else to drive him. So Fermi drove, and Baudino sat facing the rear, so that he could see the license plates of cars behind them. Any car that seemed to follow them would arouse suspicion, and Baudino would tell Fermi to take evasive action. The two became good friends. As a law school graduate, Baudino gave legal advice to anyone needing it. He sometimes helped out with simple tasks in the laboratory to pass the time.

On November 16, 1942, construction of the Chicago pile began. A reactor would show whether a chain reaction could be achieved in the laboratory and whether it could be made self-sustaining. If so, perhaps the released energy could be harnessed into a bomb.

CHAPTER EIGHT

CHICAGO AND LOS ALAMOS

Because the pile at Columbia could not be built higher than the ceiling, Fermi thought perhaps removing the air from it would improve its performance. Air trapped in the graphite was probably absorbing some of the neutrons. So Fermi ordered metal sections to be prepared and connected, to enclose the entire room. The air was then pumped out. This did have an effect on the loss of neutrons, but not a great one.[1] Fermi then considered pumping in methane, a light combustible gas. But methane when mixed with air could explode, so Fermi gave up on this idea.

He thought removing the air might work on the larger pile in Chicago. A metal enclosure would be impractical, but building the pile inside a giant balloon would probably work. So a huge square balloon was ordered from the Goodyear Tire and Rubber Company.[2] When the balloon arrived, Fermi stationed himself on a movable platform high above the floor. As he shouted orders to the men below, the balloon was hoisted into place. One flap was left open, and through this the material was assembled. First came the blocks of wood that would support the pile. Next came the graphite bricks. The pile was to be a sphere about 26 feet in diameter. Each layer was put in place after discussions with Fermi and extensive calculations. Most of the uranium lumps were placed in the center, with others distributed in the graphite. Then it was found that a vacuum was not necessary, and so the balloon was never sealed.[3]

To control the reaction, cadmium sheets nailed to wooden rods were inserted into the pile. Cadmium is a metallic element that was known to be a strong neutron absorber. The movable rods were locked into position at night. Each day they were removed and the reactivity of the pile was measured. From the neutron intensity measured, the scientists could calculate how much material had to be added to reach critical size—that is, how much was needed to make the reaction self-sustaining.

As each shift reported the neutron level to Fermi, he pulled out his slide rule—the common way to do quick calculations in the days before electronic calculators—to figure how close they were to a chain reaction. His calculations showed that with the fifty-seventh layer, the pile would become self-sustaining. This layer was to be added during the night shift of December 1–2, 1942, but Fermi ordered a delay until morning.

Safety measures were important. A control rod was

arranged that would automatically fall and shut down the reaction if the neutron intensity got too high. As backup, another control rod hung by a rope over the reactor. It could be cut down quickly, if necessary. As a last resort, three men stood by with buckets of cadmium sulfate. They were to dump the buckets' contents if a dangerous runaway reaction should occur.

On the morning of December 2, about forty persons were assembled to witness the first controlled man-made self-sustaining nuclear chain reaction. Among those on the spectators' balcony was Crawford H. Greenewalt of the DuPont Company. DuPont was being urged by the Army to build and operate reactors. Greenewalt was invited to be present to help him decide on the Army's proposal.

A young physicist named George Weil stood alone on the floor near a cadmium rod. His job was to pull out that rod a little at a time when Fermi told him to. All the other rods were already pulled out.

Fermi explained each step to a silent audience. "This pen will trace a line indicating the intensity of the radiation. When the pile chain-reacts, the pen will trace a line that will go up and up and that will not tend to level off. . . . Weil will first set the rod at thirteen feet. This means that thirteen feet of the rod will still be inside the pile. The counters will click faster and the pen will move up to this point, and then its trace will level off. Go ahead, George!"

Everything happened as Fermi predicted. The counters

clicked madly, the pen went up and then stopped. Fermi grinned. The audience was impressed. To make sure that nothing would disturb the experiment, Fermi wanted to reach the critical point very slowly. After all, his team was working with the unknown. There was always the possibility that they had overlooked something.

By the end of the morning, Fermi, always a creature of habit, announced, "Let's go to lunch." To him, nothing was important enough to interfere with lunchtime. The control rods were locked in place when everyone left for lunch. After lunch, the group reassembled. They waited, full of suspense. The control rods were brought out slowly. Fermi's eyes flew from the recording pen to his slide rule and back. "Pull it out another foot," he said to Weil. At last, turning to the balcony, he announced with a smile, "This will do it. Now the pile will chain-react."[4]

> *While all eyes remained on the recording instruments, the chain reaction continued for twenty-eight minutes.*

The counters clicked, and the pen traced a line. But this time it did not level off. While all eyes remained on the recording instruments, the chain reaction continued for twenty-eight minutes. Then the pile was shut down. A bottle of wine was produced to celebrate the occasion, and everybody drank from paper cups.

Other problems now had to be solved. What was the best material to cool a reactor? What was the effect of impurities in the graphite? A larger pile was built at

Argonne that was to answer many of these questions. This led to the construction of large production reactors by the DuPont Company at the Hanford, Washington, site. Fermi traveled now and then to Hanford. His administrative duties increased.

Among the Chicago scientists, a feeling of worry and apprehension grew. What would come out of the development of atomic energy? What consequences would it bring into the world? Many scientists felt they had unleashed a monster. Niels Bohr in a private conversation

FIFTEEN YEARS AFTER ENRICO FERMI'S CHAIN-REACTION EXPERIMENT, ARTIST GARY SHEEHAN CAPTURED THE EVENT IN THIS PAINTING. FOR SECURITY REASONS, NO PHOTOGRAPHERS HAD BEEN ALLOWED AT THE ORIGINAL EVENT IN 1942.

in February 1944 stated that atomic energy "might be one of the greatest boons to mankind or might become the greatest disaster."[5]

The problem of how to actually build a bomb remained. A new laboratory would have to be built to assemble it. A site at Los Alamos in New Mexico was chosen, in a building that had housed a boarding school for boys. It was on a plateau 7,700 feet above sea level and was surrounded by mountains, pine woods, and meadows bordering the Rio Grande River.[6] The nearest city, Santa Fe, was thirty-five miles away. Secrecy, of course, was of the greatest importance, so the isolation of the site made it ideal. The beauty of the area, with its streams for fishing, wildflowers, mountain trails, and Indian ruins was sure to appeal to the scientists and other personnel.

General Groves appointed Robert Oppenheimer director of the new lab at Los Alamos. Oppenheimer was a physics professor at Berkeley, California, where he had built up a flourishing department of theoretical physics. His interests also included philosophy and politics. Some coworkers considered him arrogant, but he was brilliant and always on top of technical details. He quickly mastered the administrative duties of the new job.

About thirty scientists formed the nucleus of the staff. Here Fermi met many old friends. One was Hans Bethe, a German physicist who had studied in Rome, left Germany for England, and then taught at Cornell University in New York before joining the Los Alamos group. He was in the habit of tackling a problem all at once. Fermi showed him how to separate a problem into small steps, and how plain reasoning might lead one at least to a general solution, if not an exact one.[7] Bethe's division was charged with the design of the bomb and other properties based on theoretical studies.

Another old friend was the Hungarian Edward Teller. He and Fermi had met earlier in Rome, and again in 1937 when both were lecturing at Stanford University in California. After the university's summer session, Fermi, Teller, and Teller's wife had driven east together. Their friendship grew, as they enjoyed bouncing ideas off each other. Teller had had second thoughts about putting science to work for the war effort. But a speech by President Roosevelt convinced him that it was necessary.[8]

Niels Bohr also showed up at Los Alamos in late 1943, but his presence was supposed to remain a secret. Public knowledge that he was there would have let the world know that something important was going on at Los Alamos. Like the other scientists there, he was given a code name—Nicholas Baker. Fermi's code name was Eugene Farmer. It was forbidden to mention any scientist's real name. Even the wives had to be called by their husbands' code name.

The scientists at Los Alamos first had to sort out and define the problems they needed to solve. The laboratory had to measure nuclear properties of the isotopes uranium-235 and plutonium-239. Others studied methods to assemble the critical mass that was required to produce an explosion. Fermi's advice was invaluable in guiding the research. But he did not move to Los Alamos until August 1944. He was still needed in Chicago, and in addition he traveled occasionally to Oak Ridge and to Hanford for consultation.

Upon his arrival at Los Alamos, Fermi needed an official title. He became associate director of the laboratory and head of a new division. His division was to investigate problems that did not fit into other divisions.

THE LOS ALAMOS SCIENTISTS STAND TOGETHER FOR A GROUP PHOTOGRAPH. ENRICO FERMI IS THE THIRD FROM THE LEFT, FRONT ROW.

But being a general adviser did not satisfy Fermi. He wanted a project of his own. Therefore he became active in the group building a homogeneous nuclear reactor. This reactor consisted of a one-foot diameter sphere containing a solution of a uranium salt in water. Fermi often went to the reactor site in a nearby canyon to carry out experiments and calculations.

Another associate director was Samuel K. Allison, who had been at the Metallurgical Laboratory in Chicago. He was the kind of man that could mediate discussions and calm people down when they got too tense. He became Fermi's good friend.

General Groves referred to his scientists as "crackpots," but he meant it in an affectionate way. Fermi rejected Groves' lumping all scientists into one classification. "I am an exception," he told his wife. "I am perfectly normal."[9]

Fermi enjoyed his work at Los Alamos. Whenever any physicist ran into trouble, he could go to Fermi. More often than not, Fermi offered substantial help. He spent his after-work hours visiting with friends. Because of the isolation, families entertained each other. There were frequent dinner parties and card parties. On weekends, Fermi, along with others, hiked or skied in the mountains. He even took up fishing. He had certain ideas about how fish should behave, but the fish did not always follow his expectations.[10]

Life at Los Alamos was very regulated. Only authorized personnel could enter the area. Trips to Santa Fe required special permission. Large purchases could be dropped off at an office in Santa Fe, to be delivered later by truck. Upon returning from a trip to the outside, everyone had to show a badge. Mail was censored. General Groves had each scientist vouch for the loyalty of one other worker that the scientist knew well.[11]

Wives were encouraged to work. Secretaries were needed, and many wives were happy to take part in the war effort and earn a little money. Laura Fermi worked three hours each day in the medical office. There she picked up gossip about individuals, which she passed on to her husband.

Hans Bethe's wife Rose was in charge of housing assignments. The most desirable houses were those that had belonged to the Los Alamos school. Because they were the only homes with bathtubs rather than showers, this group of houses was known as "Bathtub Row." The families that lived there acquired a higher social status. They were also the ones that could hire a maid. Each morning, army buses brought in women from the surrounding villages and Indian pueblos to clean and cook for Los Alamos families.[12] Employment opportunities at Los Alamos enriched the economy for miles around.

In September of 1944 the reactor at Hanford was ready to begin operation. Fermi had to be there, in case of trouble. At that time he was in Tennessee. Sam Allison and Arthur Compton were to accompany him. The group was not allowed to fly, for safety reasons, so the three took a train. To pass the time on this long trip,

Compton posed a problem to Fermi. "When I was in the Andes Mountains on my cosmic ray trips," he said, "I noticed that at very high altitudes my watch did not keep good time." Compton asked Fermi for an explanation. Fermi took out his slide rule, found paper and pencil, and began writing out mathematical formulas. He ended his calculations with a figure telling how much the watch would slow down. It more or less matched the discrepancy that Compton remembered. He and Allison were thoroughly impressed.[13]

The Hanford reactor started according to plan, but after several days it began to slow down and then it stopped. After a few hours it started up again. What was the cause? Fermi figured out that the pile was being poisoned by a fission byproduct. This byproduct was found to be the inert gas xenon-135, a prolific neutron absorber. Once this was understood, corrections were made. Soon after, Fermi returned to Los Alamos, where another crisis awaited him.

At first a gun-like arrangement had been proposed to bring together two parts to form the critical mass that was essential for an explosion. Now it was found that this would not work. Each plutonium-239 atom produced in a pile captures a neutron to form plutonium-240. This plutonium-240 rapidly undergoes spontaneous fission. Not enough neutrons are left to cause an explosion. An alternative to the gun arrangement was needed.

A physicist named Seth Neddermeyer proposed an implosion arrangement. By this method, small explosives are arranged around a sphere. When detonated, they push together the fissionable material inside the sphere. The theoretical department did the necessary calculations. Other experts were brought in to work on the implosion technique. By the end of 1944, all problems had been resolved.

The next step was to actually build a bomb and test it. This was probably the most important physics experiment of all time. It was given the code name "Trinity." It would take place at a desert site near Los Alamos. Fermi was one of the very few persons who understood all the

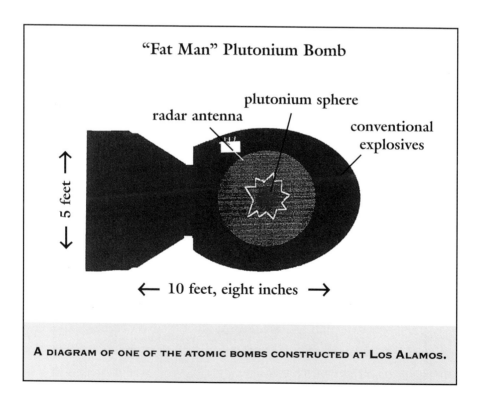

A DIAGRAM OF ONE OF THE ATOMIC BOMBS CONSTRUCTED AT LOS ALAMOS.

aspects involved in the test, which included nuclear, mechanical, thermal, optical, and geophysical factors.

On May 7, 1945, a preliminary test was done with ordinary explosives, to make sure that all the measuring instruments were working. The actual test that summer would be one that could not be repeated. Measurements would be made of the light produced, gamma rays, shock waves, and other forms of energy.

Then Germany surrendered, and the war in Europe was over. Whereas everyone was happy about this, some of the European physicists working at Los Alamos were slightly disappointed. They had hoped to have an atomic bomb ready in order to destroy the evil Nazi government of Germany. But the war with Japan still continued. Preparations to test the bomb were speeded up.

Material arrived from Oak Ridge and from Hanford, to be worked on by the Los Alamos scientists. A bomb containing plutonium-239 was to be exploded at the top of a steel tower. Scientists moved into barracks on the testing site. Fermi participated in most of the work. Everyone worked hard in the early morning, while the weather was still cool. As the temperature rose, every person's movements became sluggish. In the evening, everyone returned to their barracks.

The night before the test, a thundershower pelted the desert. But the test was not postponed. Everyone went to their preassigned posts: Fermi and Segrè were at the nine-mile mark. Those with no direct participation were twenty miles removed. Sam Allison, who was to give the countdown to detonate the bomb, was in a shelter five miles away.

At 5:30 A.M. on July 15, the bomb was exploded. The entire sky lit up with an unbelievable brightness, even for those wearing very dark glasses. Fermi got up, tore sheets of paper into small bits, and dropped them at his feet. When the shock wave arrived, it blew the bits of paper a short distance. From a measurement of this distance, Fermi was able to calculate the energy of the explosion. He was so absorbed in this simple experiment that he did not even hear the thunderous roar that followed.[14]

About an hour later, Fermi climbed into a lead-shielded tank, which took him to the site of the explosion. There he collected samples to be analyzed. The bomb had dug a huge crater in the desert. The sand in the area had melted and turned into glass.

After a day of collecting data from the various instruments, the men returned to Los Alamos. They were all exhausted. Fermi went to bed without a word. He had been too tired to drive back himself, and was happy, for once, to leave the driving to someone else.

CHAPTER NINE

AFTER THE WAR

The bomb test had been wildly successful. It was a source of pride to all concerned. The general feeling was that now the war with Japan would surely end soon. But at the same time, doubt and worry crept into the minds of the scientists. What would be the future of atomic energy? Could it be used for the benefit of mankind, or only for destruction? Each of the scientists brought his own beliefs and experiences to this issue.

In science, problems are almost always clearly defined, and theories can be tested and confirmed by experiments. In politics and social issues, this is not so. In spite of feelings of guilt among some scientists, there was also hope. There will be no more wars, they said. Atomic power will be used for peaceful purposes only. There will be international cooperation, and each country's atomic research facilities will be open to inspection. Who could possibly object to such a program?

Fermi did not agree with these views. He pointed to the examples of history: The improvements of weapons had never kept men from waging war. He felt the world was not ready for the mutual trust that would be necessary, or for any form of world government.[1] But he did not express these views publicly.

Even before the bomb test, the scientists who were most deeply concerned about the uses of atomic energy wrote letters and visited politicians. Fermi was placed on a committee to discuss and explore lines of action. He was aware that in politics, unlike in science, his abilities were limited. Action from the U.S. president was needed, but President Roosevelt had died suddenly in April 1945. The new president, Harry Truman, appointed a committee to recommend action. A scientific advisory panel for this committee consisted of Fermi, Compton, Oppenheimer, and Ernest O. Lawrence. Lawrence was one of the scientists who had worked on the separation of uranium isotopes. These four men had the responsibility of making technical recommendations regarding the military use of the bomb against Japan. The final decision rested with the President.

The panel of scientists submitted three reports to the full committee in the middle of June 1945. Two of these reports dealt with government funding of research and continuation of the engineering group that worked on applications of atomic energy. The third and most important report discussed whether a demonstration bomb should be exploded at an isolated place. Observers from a number of countries would be on hand to view the power of such a bomb. The alternate plan was to use a bomb against Japan, to bring the war quickly to an end. The panel leaned toward the second choice.[2] President Truman felt that without the bomb, the American army would have to invade Japan, with great loss of life. In order to avoid this, he ordered the bomb to be dropped on two Japanese cities, Hiroshima and Nagasaki. Japan surrendered shortly afterward.

Fermi was now faced with a personal decision. Where should he go after finishing the work at Los Alamos? Ultimately, he decided to go back to Chicago.

Arthur Compton wanted to establish three new Institutes for Basic Research at the University of Chicago. He and two associates had traveled to Santa Fe in the spring of 1945 to consult with Fermi, Samuel Allison, and Cyril S. Smith of the Los Alamos staff. Since the three from Chicago had no clearance to enter the Los Alamos area, Santa Fe was as close as they could get. Over lunch on a terrace overlooking the desert, the six men discussed the new institutes. One would deal with nuclear physics, one with applications of radioactivity in biology and medicine, and the third with the study of metals. Fermi was offered the director's post for the physics institute, but he declined.[3] He did not want to be bothered with administrative work. Samuel Allison was persuaded to take that position.

The three Chicagoans returned from this meeting and found out that just a few days before, the other three at

A MUSHROOM CLOUD FORMS ABOVE HIROSHIMA, JAPAN, AS A RESULT OF
THE FIRST ATOMIC BOMB DROPPED ON AUGUST 6, 1945.

Los Alamos had taken part in Trinity, the testing of the bomb. But they had acted so calmly, as though nothing special had happened! If they had had an urge to tell about the test, they certainly resisted it![4]

Allison, exercising his new authority, emphasized that a free exchange of information was necessary. Scientists were no longer willing to work in the secrecy that the military demanded. They were strongly in favor of civilian control of atomic energy. The military, on the other hand, stressed national security and the importance of guarding "atomic secrets."[5]

Fermi was drawn into this controversy. He felt secrecy would hinder progress in physics and related fields. He hoped for international agreement on the uses of atomic energy. To balance the need for secrecy with the need to inform the public, the U.S. government released a semi-technical report in August 1945. "It is hoped men of science in this country can use [this report] to help their fellow citizens in reaching wise decisions."[6] Congress finally passed a law calling for a civilian Atomic Energy Commission of five individuals and two advisory boards. One advisory board would be composed of scientists and engineers, and the other of military men.

Fermi served on the scientific advisory board from January 1947 to August 1950. He went to Washington about every other month for meetings that lasted two to four days. Preparation for each meeting took much of his time. He always took an active part in the discussions and made many valuable suggestions. One of his most important suggestions was that a worldwide network should be set up to detect nuclear weapons testing by other countries.[7]

Fermi and his family had left Los Alamos on New Year's Eve 1945 and returned to Chicago. They regretted parting with the many friends they had made. But they had old friends in Chicago, too. Fermi was happy to return to teaching. As always, he enjoyed interacting with young people. Some of the younger physicists from Los Alamos had been invited to join the staff of Chicago's new Institute for Nuclear Studies. Others came who were attracted by Fermi's reputation.

Besides teaching and supervising research, Fermi also held two weekly meetings with advanced students. Here he could speak with authority on any subject that came up and was remotely connected with physics. The students learned that "physics should not be a specialist's subject; physics is to be built from the ground up, brick by brick, layer by layer. . . . Abstractions come after detailed foundation work, not before."[8] Fermi dreamed of someday teaching physics to students throughout their university education, starting with a beginner's course.

In March 1946, Fermi and four other scientists were awarded the Congressional Medal for Merit for their work in developing the atomic bomb. General Groves presented the medals to Fermi, Samuel Allison, Cyril S. Smith, Robert S. Stone, and Harold C. Urey in a ceremony at the University of Chicago. Fermi's citation read:

Dr. Enrico Fermi for exceptionally meritorious conduct in the performance of outstanding service to the War Department, in accomplishments involving great responsibility and scientific distinction in connection with the development of the greatest military weapon of all time, the atomic bomb. As the pioneer who was the first man in all the world to achieve nuclear chain reaction, and as Associate Director of the Los Alamos Laboratory . . . his essential experimental work and consulting service involved great responsibility and scientific distinction. A great experimental physicist, Dr. Fermi's sound scientific judgment, his initiative and resourcefulness, and his unswerving devotion to duty have contributed vitally to the success of the Atomic Bomb Project.[9]

A new building for the institutes was constructed on the University of Chicago campus in 1947. Fermi moved into his office as soon as the wing for nuclear studies was completed. In his filing cabinets he kept what he called his "artificial memory." This was an accumulation of data, calculations, and other documents, which he had carefully indexed in a notebook. Whenever a particular bit of information was needed, he could look in his notebook and produce it within a few seconds.[10]

During the late 1940s many universities built accelerators, in which particles could be slammed into a target at incredible speeds. The Chicago physicists were eager to have one of their own. Construction of their cyclotron began in July 1947, but it would be four years before it was ready for use. It was built on the campus, deep below street level, so that any stray radiation would be absorbed by the ground. For extra protection, it was enclosed in a thick shield of concrete. Fermi looked forward eagerly to its completion, the way a child looks forward to a promised toy. In the meantime he did theoretical work on particle physics.

One question that held Fermi's interest was: What holds a nucleus together? Protons, being positively charged, should repel one another. A Japanese physicist, Hideki Yukawa, had suggested the existence of a new particle that serves to hold the nucleus together, like a sort of glue. Studies of cosmic rays showed the existence of these strange new particles. They are formed when cosmic rays collide with atoms in the earth's atmosphere.

> *"Physics should not be a specialist's subject. . . . Abstractions come after detailed foundation work, not before."*
> —Enrico Fermi

They were called mesons, meaning middle particles, because their mass is between that of a proton and an electron. But it turned out there are different kinds of mesons. The kind that interested Fermi are called pi-mesons, or pions.

To study these new particles, accelerators were built to give known particles like protons and neutrons energy comparable to cosmic rays. Theoretically, since mass and energy are interchangeable (as was first shown by Einstein), if enough energy is available, it should be possible to create particles. This does actually happen in giant accelerators. But such "virtual" particles live for only tiny fractions of a second. They can be detected only through their effect on "real" particles.

The Chicago cyclotron consists of a huge 2200-ton magnet, as tall as a small house, and a metal box. The metal box is emptied of air by nine vacuum pumps. The particles to be accelerated are sent into the box. The magnet bends their path to keep them inside the box. An electric current is sent through copper coils wound around a steel core, to magnetize the core. The coils are hollow to let water circulate through them, in order to cool the copper. A concrete wall surrounds the cyclotron, with a doorway in it. The cyclotron shuts off automatically if this doorway is open. There are also other safety features to protect workers.

Fermi added one part to the cyclotron. He made the target movable so that the cyclotron need not be stopped if the target had to be moved. A platform on four wheels, now called "Fermi's trolley," holds the target and can be moved to any point along the rim of the magnet by a controller in another room.

Fermi had long been interested in cosmic rays. Now, with the cyclotron, he extended the work done by others in this field, and made some important contributions. He developed a statistical theory of the interaction between mesons and protons. His calculations led to a certain ratio between various interactions, which was confirmed through experiments.[11] Computers were now coming into use, and they made carrying out the complicated calculations much easier.

A new reactor had been built at the Argonne Laboratory. This one used heavy water as a moderator. In heavy water, the hydrogen atom has both a proton and a neutron instead of only a proton. With neutrons produced in this reactor, Fermi began a new series of experiments. In one approach, neutrons were treated as a stream of particles. In another approach, they were treated as a mixture of waves. They could be separated according to wavelength, just like light can be separated into a rainbow of colors. Also, they could be separated according to their energy level. The way these neutrons were absorbed or scattered by target materials gave Fermi insight into the structure of a nucleus. In his experiments, Fermi borrowed from the techniques and theory that had been developed in studying light and X-rays. His methods showed that there is a unity of physics in all these phenomena.

As was his custom, Fermi spent his summers away from the university. Other universities competed to have him come and give lectures. The Italian Accademia dei Lincei also sponsored him in a series of lectures. The Academia had been disbanded by the Fascists in 1939, but was now reorganized. A new generation of Italian physicists, who were just beginning their own research, flocked to hear Fermi's simple explanations of the latest developments in their field.

In 1945 Fermi had proudly become a U.S. citizen. He embraced enthusiastically the democracy of the United States. Now, in the early 1950s, he was again drawn into public affairs.

CHAPTER TEN

FERMI'S LEGACY

$\mathbf{T}$he political climate in the U.S. in the postwar years was one of distrust. America's recent ally, the Soviet Union, had forced several Eastern European countries to adopt the Soviet style of Communism, a totalitarian form of government. In the 1950s the Soviet Union tried to extend its influence even farther into Europe and Asia. There was widespread fear that the Soviets had the knowledge necessary to build an atomic bomb, and might decide to use one.

In the U.S., Julius and Ethel Rosenberg were put on trial for passing secret information about the atomic bomb to the Soviets, convicted, and put to death. The German physicist Klaus Fuchs, who had worked at Los Alamos, was likewise tried for spying, and sentenced to a long imprisonment. Even one of Fermi's co-workers, Bruno Pontecorvo, disappeared in 1950 or 1951, and was believed to have gone to the Soviet Union.

Fortunately, he did not have any important secret information.[1]

Scientists and others who had a part in the atomic bomb project were now under suspicion. Who else might have passed on secrets to the Russians? Even J. Robert Oppenheimer, the director of Los Alamos, was accused of spying. This of course bothered Fermi greatly. Hearings were held in the spring of 1954. Fermi testified in support of Oppenheimer. He stated that he himself always supported and agreed with "Oppie's" decisions and recommendations. But there were others who cast doubt on Oppenheimer's loyalty. In the end he was denied further security clearance by a vote of two to one.

Fermi was elected president of the American Physical Society in 1953. As its spokesman, he was involved in another controversy. This one pitted the Secretary of Commerce in President Eisenhower's cabinet against the National Bureau of Standards, an agency whose function is to verify scientific and technical claims of products. The Secretary, under political pressure, had overruled the Bureau in one of its findings. Fermi issued a statement that "it is the duty of a scientist to investigate scientific and technical problems by openly-stated objective methods without shading his conclusion under political or other pressures." His statement urged that the government should proclaim that "this principle forms the rule of ethics for scientists in government service and that no scientist will be penalized for adhering to them."[2]

In the early 1950s, the question of compensating the

discoverers of the effect of slow neutrons arose. The U.S. government had made extensive use of the patent that Fermi and his six assistants had taken out in both Italy and the U.S. in the mid-1930s. Fermi would have given up his rights to compensation, but he felt he needed to protect the rights of the other six. In the end, each inventor received, after legal expenses, $20,000.[3]

In the summer of 1953, Fermi returned to Los Alamos to use the laboratory's computer to analyze results of his experiments with pi-mesons. Segrè visited him in Chicago in February 1954, and they discussed the polarization of protons in high-energy scattering experiments (analogous to the polarization of light, in which the waves are confined to one plane in space). Fermi worked out the math in two hours at his office blackboard. This became the basis of one of his last publications.

In the summer of 1954 Fermi again went to Europe. He had prepared a course on pions and other nuclear particles for the summer school of the Italian Physical Society. He hiked in the mountains, an activity he had always loved, but he did not have his usual stamina. Back in Chicago, a check-up at the hospital showed he had stomach cancer—a possible result of his work with radioactive substances. An exploratory operation revealed he did not have long to live. He remained in the hospital, hooked up to a nutrient solution dripping into his veins. In typical fashion, he timed the drops and calculated the rate of flow, just like in one of his

FERMI AT THE UNIVERSITY OF CHICAGO, CIRCA 1947.

experiments.[4] He still hoped to write a textbook on nuclear physics. Unfortunately he did not live long enough. He died on November 29, 1954, two months after his fifty-third birthday.

Enrico Fermi was no doubt one of the greatest scientific minds of the twentieth century. For twenty-five years he dominated the field of physics. His work greatly advanced scientists' understanding of certain phenomena of the natural world. He brought honor, first to his native land by leading Italy into a prominent position in the world of physics, and later, to the United States.

His most important contributions are:

1. Fermi statistics (also developed by Paul Dirac), which explain how electrons move in metals, how their behavior in an atom can be explained, and how that behavior affects a large assembly of atoms.

2. The beta-decay theory, which Fermi considered his greatest achievement. This was a mathematical explanation of what makes a neutron split into a proton and an electron. It introduced the "weak force" as one of the four fundamental forces of the natural world.

3. His studies and explanations of neutron physics, especially the discovery of the effect of slow neutrons, which led to the formation of new elements and the discovery of fission. This was the principal work that earned him the Nobel Prize.

4. The achievement of a controlled self-sustaining chain reaction. This led to the development of a new source of energy and was the decisive factor that brought an end

to World War II. In most people's minds, this is what Enrico Fermi is remembered for.

The Fermi name is attached to a number of items in the world of physics, as well as to several institutions. Electrons, protons, and neutrons are collectively called fermions, because they behave according to the statistics worked out by Fermi and Dirac.

The unit of length of a proton or neutron, which can be represented by a decimal point followed by eleven zeros and a one, or one-trillionth of a centimeter, is called a fermi. The element of atomic number 100, which was discovered in 1952, has been named fermium.

The accelerator laboratory built in the late 1960s in Batavia, Illinois, near Chicago, is called the Fermi National Accelerator Laboratory, or Fermilab for short. The Institute for Nuclear Studies which Fermi headed in Chicago after leaving Los Alamos is now named The Enrico Fermi Institute. Likewise, the Italian Physical Society's summer school where Fermi lectured is now named after him.

Fermi's published papers were eventually collected and republished in two volumes.[5]

Just before Fermi's death, the Atomic Energy Commission gave him a special award of $25,000 for his achievements. Later awards from the AEC were named the Fermi Prize. It is given each year "to recognize someone of international esteem, whose career has been marked by continued exceptional contributions to the development, use, or control of nuclear energy." In 1963 it was awarded to J. Robert Oppenheimer.

Being a genius in any field does not necessarily make one a great human being. There have been instances of such individuals who were not at all nice or kind. But this was not true of Fermi. He was modest, conscientious, kind, disciplined, and helpful to others. He felt he was blessed with special talents, and he used his mental gifts for a better understanding of the physical world. He truly enjoyed teaching. The study of physics became exciting for his students. Each one could feel fortunate and honored to have been associated with such a great physicist and a great man.

Since Fermi's time, larger accelerators have been built, and new particles have been detected in recent years. Fermi would have been excited about the latest discoveries. He realized that every time physicists answer one question, more questions present themselves. Much like a nuclear reaction, it seems that the mysteries of science are self-sustaining.

ACTIVITIES

Activity One: Estimating Numbers

Fermi loved to estimate figures by making a few assumptions, even for problems that had nothing to do with physics. A typical problem might be: How many barbers can a city of 500,000 support?

Assume half the population is men and boys, and they visit a barber on the average of once a month. Of the 250,000, assume 10% are either babies or men who wear their hair long. That leaves 225,000 who need haircuts. Assume a barber can do 24 cuts a day, and he works 22 days out of a month. The city then could use 225,000 divided by 528 (24 x 22), or 426, barbers.

Activity Two: Transfer of Energy

Line up five pennies on a smooth surface so that they are touching one another. Now move the first penny a few inches away, and flick it towards the second penny. What happens? What does this show about the energy you gave the first penny? The same thing can happen to particles in an atomic nucleus.

Place a baseball or small rubber ball in a plastic bag. Swing the bag in big circles over your head. Let go suddenly. Measure how far the bag travels before it stops by counting the steps you need to take. Now repeat, but this time swing the bag faster and faster before letting go. How much farther did the bag go?

The energy of your swinging arm was transferred to the ball inside the bag. This is the principle of the cyclotron. If the ball was an atomic particle, it could have smashed into something with all the energy the cyclotron had given it.

Activity Three: Set Up a Chain Reaction

Stand up dominoes on their narrow end, one in the first row, then two dominoes side by side, about two inches away, placed so that when the first one falls, it will make the next two fall. In the third row place four dominoes side by side, again two inches away from the second row. In the fourth row, place eight dominoes side by side. When the first domino is pushed down, it will make the second, third, and fourth rows fall down in turn. This is a chain reaction. The dominoes represent neutrons released by uranium atoms.

CHRONOLOGY

1901—Born in Rome, Italy, September 29.

1915—Brother, Giulio, dies.

1918—Admitted to the Scuola Normale Superiore in Pisa, and also enrolls at the University of Pisa.

1921—Publishes first scientific paper.

1922—Earns doctor's degree from the University of Pisa.

1923—Postdoctoral study at the University of Göttingen, Germany.

1924—Teaching assistant at the University of Rome; three-month assistantship at Leyden, The Netherlands.

1925—Teaches at the University of Florence; does first experimental work.

1926—Describes mathematically the behavior of electrons (Fermi-Dirac statistics); appointed professor at the University of Rome.

1928—Marries Laura Capon, July 19.

1930—First trip to the U.S.; lectures at the University of Michigan.

1933—Works out the theory of beta-decay.

1934—Carries out experiments on inducing radioactivity by means of neutron bombardment; discovers effect of slow neutrons.

1938—Awarded Nobel Prize in physics; emigrates to the U.S.

1939—Research on chain reaction at Columbia University.

1941—U.S. enters World War II.

1942—Moves research to Chicago; achieves first sustained chain reaction on December 2.

1944—Moves to Los Alamos.

1945—First atomic bomb tested; World War II ends after two atomic bombs are dropped on Japan.

1946—Joins new Institute for Nuclear Physics in Chicago.

1947—Serves on General Advisory Committee of
-1950 Atomic Energy Commission.

1951—Begins experiments using new Chicago cyclotron.

1954—Dies on November 29 of cancer.

CHAPTER NOTES

Chapter 1. What's Inside an Atom?

1. Isaac Asimov, *Atom* (New York: Penguin Books USA Inc., 1991), p. 17.

2. Emilio Segrè, *Enrico Fermi, Physicist* (Chicago: University of Chicago Press, 1970), pp. 215–216.

3. H. Pleijel, Introductory speech at Nobel Prize ceremony.

Chapter 2. Early Years

1. Emilio Segrè, *Enrico Fermi, Physicist* (Chicago: University of Chicago Press, 1970), p. 4.

2. Laura Fermi, *Atoms in the Family* (Chicago: University of Chicago Press, 1954), p. 15.

3. Ibid., p. 13.

4. Segrè, p. 5.

5. Rachel Fermi, personal communication with author, November 5, 2002.

6. Segrè, p. 7.

7. Laura Fermi, p. 19.

8. Segrè, p. 10.

9. Richard Rhodes, *The Making of the Atomic Bomb* (New York: Simon & Schuster Inc., 1986), p. 205.

Chapter 3. Preparing for a Career

1. Emilio Segrè, *Enrico Fermi, Physicist* (Chicago: University of Chicago Press, 1970), p. 15.

2. Laura Fermi, *Atoms in the Family* (Chicago: University of Chicago Press, 1954), p. 22.

3. Ibid., p. 24.

4. Segrè, p. 18.

5. Ibid., p. 21.

6. Laura Fermi, p. 26.

7. Segrè, p. 24.

8. Laura Fermi, p. 30.

9. Ibid., p. 35.

10. McGraw-Hill Encyclopedia of Science & Technology, Vol. 7, p. 51.

11. Segrè, p. 45.

Chapter 4. Bringing Modern Physics to Italy

1. Laura Fermi, *Atoms in the Family* (Chicago: University of Chicago Press, 1954), p. 3.

2. Ibid., p. 52.

3. Ibid., p. 59.

4. Ibid., pp. 46–47.

5. Emilio Segrè, *Enrico Fermi, Physicist* (Chicago: University of Chicago Press, 1970), p. 54.

6. Segrè, p. 60.

7. Laura Fermi, p. 71.

8. Ibid., p. 71.

9. Ibid., p. 78.

Chapter 5. Experiments on Atomic Nuclei

1. Emilio Segrè, *Enrico Fermi, Physicist* (Chicago: University of Chicago Press, 1970), p. 66.

2. Isaac Asimov, *New Intelligent Man's Guide to Science, Vol. I* (New York: Basic Books Inc., 1965), p. 264.

3. Necia H. Apfel, *It's All Elementary* (New York: Lothrop Lee & Shepard Books, 1985), p. 86.

4. Laura Fermi, *Atoms in the Family* (Chicago: University of Chicago Press, 1954), p. 87.

5. Ibid., p. 91.

6. Ibid.

7. Ibid., p. 92.

8. Segrè, p. 80.

9. Laura Fermi, p. 99–100.

10. Segrè, p. 90.

Chapter 6. Momentous Changes

1. Laura Fermi, *Atoms in the Family* (University of Chicago Press, 1954), p. 118.
2. Ibid., p. 114.
3. Ibid., p. 120.
4. Ibid., p. 115.
5. Ibid., p. 124.
6. Ibid., p. 120.
7. Ibid., p. 128.
8. Ibid., p. 130.
9. Ibid., p. 134.
10. Ibid., p. 133.

Chapter 7. The War Effort

1. Emilio Segrè, *Enrico Fermi, Physicist* (University of Chicago Press, 1970), p. 105.
2. Ibid., p. 107.
3. Richard Rhodes, *The Making of the Atomic Bomb* (Simon & Schuster Inc., 1986), p. 313.
4. Laura Fermi, *Atoms in the Family* (University of Chicago Press, 1954), p. 158.
5. Segrè, p. 110.
6. Ibid., p. 103.
7. Rhodes, p. 301.
8. Segrè, p. 116.
9. Ibid., p. 117.
10. Laura Fermi, p. 168.
11. Ibid., p. 169.
12. Ibid., p. 173.
13. Segrè, p. 127.

Chapter 8. Chicago and Los Alamos

1. Laura Fermi, *Atoms in the Family* (University of Chicago Press, 1954), p. 186.
2. Ibid., p. 192.

3. Ibid., p. 194.

4. Ibid., pp. 196–197.

5. Richard Rhodes, *The Making of the Atomic Bomb* (New York: Simon & Schuster Inc. 1986), p. 526.

6. Emilio Segrè, *Enrico Fermi, Physicist* (Chicago: University of Chicago Press, 1970), p. 133.

7. Laura Fermi, p. 217.

8. Ibid., p. 220.

9. Ibid., p. 226.

10. Segrè, p. 140.

11. Emilio Segrè, *A Mind Always in Motion* (Berkeley, Calif.: University of California Press, 1993), p. 183.

12. Laura Fermi, p. 231.

13. Segrè, *Enrico Fermi, Physicist*, p. 143.

14. Laura Fermi, p. 239.

Chapter 9. After the War

1. Laura Fermi, *Atoms in the Family* (University of Chicago Press, 1954), p. 246.

2. Emilio Segrè, *Enrico Fermi, Physicist* (University of Chicago Press, 1970), p. 154.

3. Ibid., p. 156.

4. Laura Fermi, p. 248.

5. Segrè, p. 158.

6. Ibid., p. 160.

7. Ibid., pp. 164–165.

8. Segrè, p. 170.

9. Laura Fermi, p. 249.

10. Segrè, p. 173.

11. Laura Fermi, pp. 260–261.

Chapter 10. Fermi's Legacy

1. Laura Fermi, *Atoms in the Family* (University of Chicago Press, 1954), p. 255.

2. Emilio Segrè, *Enrico Fermi, Physicist* (University of Chicago Press, 1970), p. 180.

3. Emilio Segrè, *A Mind Always in Motion* (Berkeley, Calif.: University of California Press, 1993), p. 246.

4. Emilio Segrè, *Enrico Fermi, Physicist*, p. 184.

5. Emilio Segrè, *A Mind Always in Motion*, p. 268.

GLOSSARY

accelerator—A device to bring charged particles up to high speeds and energies.

alpha particle—A positively charged particle given off by the nucleus of an atom during nuclear transformation.

atomic number—The number of protons in one atom of a particular element.

atoms—The particles that make up the basic chemical elements.

beryllium—A light-weight metallic element of atomic number 4.

beta-decay—The breakdown of a nucleus of an atom to produce a high-speed electron.

beta particle—An electron given off by the nucleus of an atom during nuclear transformation.

chain reaction—A series of events where each action initiates the next.

critical mass—The minimum amount of fissionable material that will sustain a nuclear chain reaction.

cyclotron—A circular type of particle accelerator.

electrons—Subatomic particles with a negative charge that orbit the nucleus of an atom.

experimentalist—A scientist who conducts experiments to gather data or test a theory. Factors that might affect the results must be carefully controlled.

fascism—A political belief or movement that stands for a strong central government and rigid control over its citizens.

fission—An energy-producing process in which atoms are split.

frequency—The number of vibrations or waves per unit of time.

gamma rays—A form of radiation similar to X-rays.

Geiger counter—A device for detecting nuclear radiation and measuring its intensity.

graphite—A crystalline form of carbon, used to moderate chain reactions.

isotope—One of several forms of the same element. It has a different number of neutrons than the most common form of that element but the same number of protons.

magnetic field—The region around a permanent magnet or around a conductor carrying an electric current.

moderator—The material in a nuclear reactor that reduces the speed of high-energy neutrons.

Nazi government—The government of Germany under the dictator Adolf Hitler, governing from 1933 to 1945.

neptunium—A radioactive metallic element of atomic number 93, formed by the bombardment of uranium-238 with neutrons.

neutrons—Subatomic particles that carry no charge. Along with protons, they make up the nucleus of an atom.

nucleus—The central part of an atom, containing protons and neutrons.

paraffin—A waxy material containing carbon and hydrogen.

periodic chart or periodic table—A chart of the chemical elements, arranged by atomic number and organized into related groups.

photon—An elementary particle or packet of energy in

which light and other forms of electromagnetic radiation are emitted.

pile—A nuclear reactor.

plutonium—A radioactive element of atomic number 94 that is capable of splitting into other elements.

protons—Subatomic particles that have a positive charge. Along with neutrons, they make up the nucleus of an atom.

radiation—The particles or energy given off by an atom when it is undergoing nuclear transformation.

radioactive decay—The transformation of an element due to a change in the number of protons and neutrons in its atoms.

radium—A metallic element of atomic number 88.

radon—A colorless gas of atomic number 86, formed by natural radioactive decay of radium.

relativity—The theory that expresses the equivalence between mass and energy, and the interdependence of matter, time, and space.

spectroscopy—The study of characteristic series of lines in the spectrum produced when an element is heated. It is used to identify elements in a mixture.

spectrum—The range of electromagnetic radiation, from gamma rays which have the shortest wavelength to radio waves which have the longest. Light is the visible part of the spectrum.

theoretician—A scientist who derives general principles or concepts to explain observed facts.

uranium—A radioactive metal of atomic number 92. It is the heaviest naturally-occurring element.

X-rays—A form of electromagnetic radiation.

FURTHER READING

Bankston, John. *Enrico Fermi and the Nuclear Reactor.* Bear, Del.: Mitchell Lane Publishers, 2003.

Cooper, Dan. *Enrico Fermi and the Revolution in Modern Physics.* New York: Oxford University Press, 1999.

Fox, Karen. *The Chain Reaction: Pioneers of Nuclear Science.* Danbury, Conn.: Franklin Watts, Inc., 1998.

Gilmore, Robert. *Alice in Quantumland.* New York: Copernicus/Springer-Verlag, 1995.

Gonick, Larry, and Art Huffman. *The Cartoon Guide to Physics.* New York: HarperCollins Publishers, 1990.

Hamilton, Janet. *Lise Meitner: Pioneer of Nuclear Fission.* Berkeley Heights, N.J.: Enslow Publishers, Inc., 2003.

Pasachoff, Naomi. *Niels Bohr: Physicist and Humanitarian.* Berkeley Heights, N.J.: Enslow Publishers, Inc., 2003.

INTERNET ADDRESSES

The Enrico Fermi Institute
http://efi.uchicago.edu/

Fermi Mini-Exhibit
http://www.aip.org/history/esva/exhibits/fermi.htm

Nobel Prize Home Page
http://www.nobel.se

INDEX